Am I Enough? is an honest and real account of the lies many of us believe about our worth. Grace fills her readers with truth from Jesus, allowing them to find their worth in Someone worth following.

—BOB GOFF, BESTSELLING AUTHOR OF
LOVE DOES AND *EVERYBODY, ALWAYS*

With whimsical honesty and relevant wisdom, Grace reveals in these pages the beautiful truths she's learned from hard-won experience. Truths to dispel the lies you tell yourself that shame you and prevent you from experiencing the fullness of life God has to offer. Truths to remind you that you are—finally—enough. Every girl needs a friend like Grace, and this book is the late-night girl talk you've been longing for.

—ALLISON TROWBRIDGE, AUTHOR OF *TWENTY-TWO:*
LETTERS TO A YOUNG WOMAN SEARCHING FOR MEANING

Am I Enough? shines the light of truth on the lies Satan and society tell us. Grace Valentine authentically declares where our worth comes from and points to the Lord in every line of this book. She talks about freedom that comes from the grace the Lord gives, not our efforts. I am so thankful for her ministry and her stand for Christ. This is a must read.

—EMILY ANN ROBERTS, COUNTRY MUSIC ARTIST,
RUNNER UP ON *THE VOICE* SEASON 9

I think as young women of God it is really hard to feel enough with all the worldly things around us. This book will help equip you to know that through God's eyes, you are more than enough. I am so excited to share this book with all my friends!

—BROOKE TERKEURST, INFLUENCER, FASHION BLOGGER,
AND YOUTUBER AT THE *LIVINGLOVEDVLOGS* CHANNEL

Real, relatable, relevant, and readable; *Am I Enough* shares a message for young women all over the world. Grace's honest struggle of trading wordly thinking for the truths rooted in the worthiness of Christ holds the power to transform young girls' lives everywhere and for a very long time.

—ELIZABETH VINTURELLA, BLOGGER AT *JUSTDOTODAY.ORG*,
PUBLIC SPEAKER, ENCOURAGER

Grace articulates what the next generation of young women are thinking and believing about their self-worth. I found myself nodding my head in affirmation because I, too, know what it's like to feel insufficient. *Am I Enough?* offers a heartfelt and truthful look at what God has to say about us and why we should listen up. I can't wait to give this to the women I am investing in.

—KAT ARMSTRONG, AUTHOR AND COFOUNDER OF *POLISHED*

Am I Enough? is a message everyone in our current "selfie generation" needs to hear. Grace provides her readers with a wake-up call about the lies our culture tells us about our identity, self-worth, and success—she points her readers toward a true identity found in Jesus.

—ALEX DEMCZAK, FORMER SEC QUARTERBACK, AUTHOR OF *THRIVE U*

Grace's whitty lines and authentic approach truly grabs the reader. *Am I Enough?* is packed with so much thought-provoking truth. Each chapter echoes peace in the hearts of so many! This is definitely a must read!

—YB, BOLD RECORDS RECORDINGS ARTIST, CHRISTIAN RAPPER

In this life-giving book, Grace speaks honestly and openly about finding the truth about who you are and who God created you to be. Grace has an admirable gift that will revamp your mind with a fresh version of the life you were called to live. I am so thankful and proud of this book!

—BRITTANY MERRILL, CHRISTIAN LIFESTYLE AND FASHION BLOGGER

Am I Enough? is great for women of all ages who struggle with insecurity. Grace's personality shines through her writing as she helps readers embrace their true worth. This book would be perfect to use in youth groups. As a mom, this will be a wonderful resource for my daughter as she grows up, and I can't wait to read this alongside her in her teens.

—WHITNEY ARCH, *OUR BEAUTIFUL LIFE* PARENTING BLOG

In these pages you will find encouragement, biblical truth, and a sense of belonging as you are reminded of your God-given worthiness. You will laugh, cry, and close each chapter feeling empowered and loved. I recommend this book to every young woman I know.

—MADISON WHEAT, FOUNDER AND WRITER FOR
THE *ME TOO, SISTER* CHRISTIAN COMMUNITY AND BLOG

am I

~~pretty enough~~

~~smart enough~~

~~successful enough~~

~~good enough~~

enough?

EMBRACING THE TRUTH ABOUT
WHO YOU ARE

grace valentine

W PUBLISHING GROUP

AN IMPRINT OF THOMAS NELSON

Published in Nashville, Tennessee, by W Publishing, an imprint of Thomas Nelson.

The author is represented by MacGregor Literary, Inc.

Thomas Nelson titles may be purchased in bulk for educational, business, fund-raising, or sales promotional use. For information, please e-mail SpecialMarkets@ ThomasNelson.com.

Library of Congress Control Number: 2018901259

ISBN 978-0-7852-1617-9 (softcover)
ISBN 978-0-7852-1615-5 (eBook)

Printed in the United States of America

18 19 20 21 22 LSC 10 9 8 7 6 5 4 3 2

To all my campers, the girls in the Life Group I lead, and all my little sisters. Each of our girl chats taught me more about Jesus. May you never lose your wonder and eagerness for our Lord. No matter what season of life you are in, may you always know your true worth. And never forget, I'm only a phone call away.

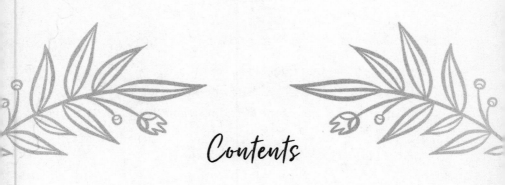

Contents

CONTENTS

Introduction

Enough!

I've had enough of trying to be good enough.

Good enough for the guy who wasn't faithful to me.

Good enough for the company that didn't offer me the summer internship of my dreams.

Good enough for the guy from my hometown who tweeted, "Why can't the girls in our town look like this?" during the Victoria's Secret Fashion Show.

I wondered what I had done wrong to make the guy unfaithful. I blamed myself and doubted my worth, assuming the other gal was prettier and cooler than me. It made me feel as if I didn't have enough to offer him.

My eyes filled with tears as I read the email informing me I hadn't landed the internship. I overanalyzed every answer I could remember giving during the interview. Obviously, whatever I said (or didn't say) wasn't good enough for them, either.

The night of that tweet, I spent three hours working out at the gym. I thought I wasn't skinny enough, and in just two months, I dropped from a size 4 to a size 0.

That was a choice I made. But as young women, we're often pushed to do everything other people want us to do. We meet the demands of our significant others in hopes of impressing them and feeling wanted. We use big words to sound smarter for the job we believe is the answer to our prayers. We count our squats in the gym and wake up earlier than we prefer so we can put on our makeup and be hot enough for the attractive guy in our chemistry lab.

We doubt our worth. We constantly play the comparison game. And for what? To find out someone else is hotter and smarter. More "enough" than we are.

The truth is, we will never be enough. We can't be enough. Not for this world anyway, because God didn't create us to please this world; He created us for His pleasure. And that creates a conflict. Both God and the world want us, but the Bible tells us that we can't belong to both.

> Do not love the world or anything in the world. If anyone loves the world, love for the Father is not in them. For everything in the world—the lust of the flesh, the lust of the eyes, and the pride of life—comes not from the Father but from the world. (1 John 2:15–16)

The line has been drawn.

Who Will You Dance With?

When I was in middle school, my mother signed me up for cotillion—which, according to the dictionary, is "a formal ball, especially one at which debutantes are presented." The experience was as awful as it sounds. I learned how to ballroom dance—the waltz, the cha-cha, the fox trot, and a number of other dances I still cannot pronounce. I received detailed instruction on dinner etiquette and how to present myself as a proper young lady. I forgot most of what I learned, but I do remember this about cotillion: we had to dance with boys.

Now that I'm a young woman, my mother wouldn't have to *make* me dance with guys. But at that stage of middle school, dancing with boys? I'd rather not. Unfortunately, my preferences were not taken into consideration.

I noticed something interesting at cotillion, though. While I was dancing, I was so focused on watching my partner's feet and following his lead that I forgot how much I hated being there.

During the Christmas ball, my partner and I competed in the cha-cha. I'm competitive, and as much as I wanted to be anywhere else, I wanted to win even more—not just for pride, but also for the prize of the most amazing popcorn anyone could ever hope to taste.

I stared so intently at my partner's feet that I saw nothing else as we danced. And we won. And my brother ate all my popcorn. (Yes, E.J., I'm still a little salty about that.)

Outside of our popcorn-winning cha-cha, dances never proved to be as fun as my mom made them sound.

God is truth, and the world tells us lies in an attempt to take us away from Him. When we fall victim to those lies—and this next "we" definitely includes me—we choose to dance with the world instead of God. Frankly, that's not a dance I enjoy.

I was thinking about cotillion and dancing the other day, and I asked myself, *Why do I follow so many things of this world that I know are not satisfying?* I keep dancing with the world. I keep danc-ing with my insecurities. My life has basically become me dancing to the wrong beat and with the wrong partner—over and over again. I've been off count, stressed, and a total mess. I've caught myself dancing to the wrong music as I worried about keeping up with a world I was not meant to keep up with. I have looked up from my feet to see I'm following the lead of my insecurities when I should be following my Creator.

I've caught myself trying to be "enough" for a partner I wasn't made to dance with.

I've heard plenty of you confess the same thoughts. Please know that we are far from alone in this struggle. We're in this together, ladies.

Can we declare together, right here, right now, that we've had enough of trying to be good enough?

Of asking:

- Am I happy enough?
- Am I loved enough?
- Am I Christian enough?
- Am I ever going to be enough?

There is One who is listening when we ask our "Am I enough?" questions. When we doubt ourselves, when we question our worth, when we ask if there's anyone out there willing to love us as we are, He answers, "I am."

God wants us to ditch the "Am I . . . ?" questions and build our lives on truth. He is offering His hand to you, hoping you will accept His offer to dance.

Lies, Lies, Lies

As young women, there are ten lies the world tells us every day. We can't truly follow the Lord's lead if we believe:

1. You are beautiful because a guy told you so.
2. Love must be earned.
3. Forget your past.
4. When you don't look "presentable," hide.
5. Numbers are the judge of beauty.
6. God just wants to be your friend.
7. Strong women cry only in the bathroom.
8. Nicholas Sparks writes the best love stories.
9. Prayer is only for when you need help.
10. You will never be enough.

Lies. All lies.

My new friend, I believe it is not coincidence that you are reading this book, because it's likely you've believed some of those lies. Maybe all of them. My purpose here is to deconstruct these ten lies and replace them with the truth God is whispering into our hearts and minds. So I'm asking you to take this journey with me.

Throughout this book, my prayer is that you are able to identify how these lies are impacting the way you view yourself and your actions. I know from experience that insecurity destroys. Insecurity crawls into our souls, seeking to steal the joy we derive from dancing with the Lord.

Spoiler alert: there is good news ahead. Grace and joy will be offered. You only have to accept.

Each of these ten lies affects you, just like they affect me. So as you explore the different sections of this book, I challenge you to read, believe, and share. Read the truth. Believe the truth, and allow it to set you free from the bondage of insecurity. Then share the truth with others who need to hear it.

Allow this book and the best love story of all time—the gospel—to change how you view yourself. Share what you read and learn with the friend who keeps wondering if her ex's new girlfriend is hotter than she is. With the friend who didn't get her dream job. And with all the women you love who need to be reminded to love themselves.

Insecurity robs women of their joy. Allow the gospel to win. Allow truth to set free those you love.

But, friend, it starts with you. Take this challenge seriously. Journal through each lie. Take time to pray after each chapter. And most important, put on your dancing shoes.

We ladies need to stick together! Treat this book as the ultimate girls' night out. Let our time together feel like 2 a.m., when you and your best friends are still wide awake, talking about life over pints of Ben & Jerry's ice cream. I promise to be honest with you, and I pray that you will be honest with yourself too.

Are you ready to dance with God instead of the world?

I am!

Real Talk

- Which of the ten lies consumes your mind the most?
- Fill in the blank: I never feel good enough for _____.
- Why are we never "enough" for this world?

- What are your goals as you read this book?
- Is there someone you would like to ask to read this book with you? Who can you partner up with to walk this journey together?
- Write a prayer to God and thank Him for being enough for you. As we move forward together, be honest about your insecurities and ask Him to remove from your thoughts the lies the world has told you.

LIE #1

You are beautiful
because a guy
told you so.

Chapter 1

Who Cares What Guys Think?

I was scrolling through my Facebook newsfeed one day in March. And for a twentysomething in March, Facebook is a parade of bikinis, girls with six-packs, and girls with six-packs next to guys with six-packs.

I found myself stalking a friend from my freshman year of college. Every spring break for the past four years, she had posted bikini pictures. I remembered that because I so desperately wanted her body. Without thinking, I typed out a message to her that day. Yes, shamefully, I admit that I messaged a thigh-gap, six-pack, bikini-confident gal showing off on Facebook—all so that I could ask how she became so skinny in the hopes of achieving the same myself.

I continued to stare at her perfect tummy and thigh gap. I needed her body.

Teach me your ways! I thought as I considered what a side-by-side photo of her and me would look like. Looking at her body, it was easy to see why so many guys like her.

I stared down to my thighs that have no gap. And my stomach

that could double as a soft, squishy pillow. I thought to myself: *It's no wonder I'm hopelessly single. But, on the bright side, without a gap, my thighs catch the french fries that miss my mouth and fall to my lap.*

I wish I could say that was the only time I'd messaged a stranger to ask how she had obtained such a glorious body. (I told you that I'd be honest with you.)

Pathetic? Yes. Normal? Most likely. Good for me? No.

We women covet the idea of being hot. We crave a great body, a beautiful face, and the ability to attract guys who deem us pretty enough by their standards. We want to feel physically attractive to and wanted by guys.

But we were meant for so much more than that. We were created for a far greater purpose than looking hot.

Out the Window

My original idea for this chapter was to ask Christian men what makes a woman beautiful, thinking it would be beneficial to hear godly men say, "Looks fade—it's all about a woman's heart and character."

This is gonna be gold! I thought when I looked over the rough outline I'd written. *Women will love this!*

I sat on my couch wearing my comfy extra-large T-shirt and loose Nike shorts, ready to send a Facebook message to the group of men I'd picked out. They were cute Christian guys who worked at summer camps and wore Chacos, and I just knew they would back me up by saying that true beauty comes from the inside.

But before I hit send, I felt God whispering to my heart, "Grace, have you not learned anything?"

What did that mean? I knew beauty comes from within. I knew our worth as women is not measured by what guys say about us or how many likes we receive on Instagram. I knew the right answer and planned on writing this truth—but also while sourcing cute, Chacos-wearing Christian guys to help get the point across and convince us women even further.

That voice I sensed in my heart asked me another question: "How would *they* know?"

I assumed these guys would be able to give answers that would help the young ladies reading this book feel better about themselves. Isn't that a sweet thought? But because I was conflicted, I did what I do quite well—I put off solving the problem. Instead, I headed over to the campus library to print a paper for my journalism class. There, I overheard two men with reputations around campus as good, Christian guys talking about two girls whom I'll call "Ashley" and "Brittany."

Good Christian Guy 1: "Did you see what Ashley was wearing last night? Her butt is honestly insane."

Good Christian Guy 2: "Yeah dude. Mind blown!"

Good Christian Guy 1: "I think she's the only hot one in that group. She's way hotter than Brittany."

Good Christian Guy 2: "Yup."

I was the one whose mind was blown. This isn't at all the view point I expected from good, Christian guys.

There went my genius plan for this chapter. Those men had failed me because they, like so many of us women, had failed to remember that a woman's worth does not lie in her looks.

When we base our worth on what the world says, it will fail us every time.

The truth is, no woman will ever be pretty enough for every

man. There will always be some guy out there who finds you unattractive.

If you put your worth in what a guy thinks of you, even if he is a Christian, I promise he will fail you. We need to stop defining our beauty by what guys think is attractive.

No More Fussing

In seventh grade, the boy sitting in the desk beside mine in English class said my arms were hairier than his. He wasn't being cruel or mean; he was just stating a fact. But when I heard him, I froze.

My brain interpreted his statement as, "Grace 'Hairy-Armed' Valentine is unworthy of being liked in seventh grade unless she shaves her arms." That night, I shaved off every hair on my arms in an attempt to alter what I perceived as a flaw in my appearance. Because of that one misplaced decision in seventh grade, I must shave my arm hair to this day or have it grow out as prickly as a cactus.

Twelve-year-old Grace allowed what I now know was a harmless comment by one guy to negatively affect my self-worth.

As I grew older, I tried to please guys through my wardrobe. I believed they would think I was hotter if I dressed more attractively. Even today, I struggle with this when I walk into my closet and feel tempted to wear a tight shirt, a short dress, or a revealing top that will catch more attention.

I'd bet some of you have also awakened in the morning and thought about dressing to please guys. But that look sends a message you probably don't intend to send.

I have a friend who was told by a guy that he would leave her if she didn't have sex with him. So she did. He still left. My friend did what she thought she had to do in order for some guy to think she was beautiful, but it still wasn't enough to keep him. And look what she gave up for nothing.

We want that guy to comment "beautiful" on our selfies. We want the hottie at the gym to say "You look good today" with his adorable smirk. Who knows? If it's a really good day, he'll wink as he says it or even offer assistance with the equipment. We want to be told that we're adorable. We want guys who don't even know our hearts to tell us that we're pretty.

But it's never enough.

This guy likes your red lipstick, that one doesn't. This guy likes you in T-shirts, that one doesn't. This guy admires that you want to wait until you're married to have sex, that one doesn't.

You might even find one guy who thinks your arms are too hairy and another who thinks it's weird that you shave them.

It's just not possible to please every guy with our looks.

Flattery isn't all that satisfying anyway. Your grandma can tell you that you're the most beautiful person in the world. Your mom can post pictures of you on Facebook and your entire hometown remarks, "Wow! She's grown up and beautiful!"

But then what? When is the next compliment coming? And what happens if it doesn't?

The problem is greater than needing a compliment or two.

We need to stop *fussing*.

One my favorite passages of Scripture is Matthew 6:25–29. The Message translation says it this way:

> If you decide for God, living a life of God-worship, it follows
> that you don't fuss about what's on the table at mealtimes or

whether the clothes in your closet are in fashion. There is far more to your life than the food you put in your stomach, more to your outer appearance than the clothes you hang on your body. Look at the birds, free and unfettered, not tied down to a job description, careless in the care of God. And you count far more to him than birds.

"Has anyone by fussing in front of the mirror ever gotten taller by so much as an inch? All this time and money wasted on fashion—do you think it makes that much difference? Instead of looking at the fashions, walk out into the fields and look at the wildflowers. They never primp or shop, but have you ever seen color and design quite like it? The ten best-dressed men and women in the country look shabby alongside them.

If you are like me and wonder what guys consider attractive and how to look better to please them—stop wondering. If you count pimples in the mirror—stop counting. If you think wearing a crop top or a sundress is the way to make guys think you are attractive—give up that idea.

Stop *fussing*.

God made you the way you are for a reason. Fussing and complaining cannot change your physical beauty.

I'm not suggesting you throw away your favorite shade of lipstick and never go to the gym again. Dress nice. Stay healthy. But don't do those things to please the world. Of course, that's not easy advice to follow, because it goes against our natural desires to please every man.

But we can't do that. And you know what? Your life serves a bigger purpose than to be eye-candy for men. When you find yourself fussing over how guys view you, pray. Take a deep breath and close Facebook. Focus on your Creator. Focus on living for the One who gave you life. Seek His eyes, and pray for the ability to see yourself the way He sees you.

You're not going to be pretty enough for the world. It's important for engaging the rest of this book to establish the fact that the world does not define us. God does. He created us, and we need to allow Him—not the temporary desires of this world—to tell us who we are.

And all God's women with or without a thigh gap said, "Amen!"

Next time you feel like fussing, step away from the mirror and go outside. Look at the wildflowers, the kittens, and the sunshine. Marvel at the mountains and the seas. God created them all. Yet *we* are His favorite creation. Celebrate that! Give Him praise through your life. Your most beautiful quality is your ability to live life purposefully.

Let's commit to spending more time clothing ourselves in the fruit of the Spirit: love, joy, peace, patience, kindness, goodness, faithfulness, gentleness, and self-control.

Let's dress ourselves with love, style ourselves with gentleness, wear self-control as though it is our favorite cross-body purse. May we choose joy daily, and throw kindness around like confetti. Let us be patient with one another and live life-bearing goodness.

Let's rock the fruits of the Spirit better than we rocked Limited Too clothes in middle school. And please, pretty please, let's wear them longer than we wore Crocs!

Real Talk

- When was the last time you fussed about the way you look? What, specifically, were you fussing about?
- Why do you think your looks are important?
- How can you remind yourself to stop fussing?
- Who determines your worth?

BOARDING PASS

TOMSON/TALIAKARIANNA

DOE 04-13-89

SEAT
33C
EXIT
MAIN 1

FLIGHT DL1693 DATE 17MAR

ORIGIN
CHICAGO-OHARE

DESTINATION
ATLANTA

OPERATED BY DELTA AIR LINES INC

DELTA (S) TSA PRECHK   BOARDING PASS

TOMSON/TALIAKARIANNA

DOE 04-13-89

H5F2Q3

NRSA

SEAT
33C
EXIT
MAIN 1

FLIGHT DL1693 DATE 17MAR CLASS J

ORIGIN
CHICAGO-OHARE

DESTINATION
ATLANTA

DEPARTS 1219P

BRD TIME 1139A

OPERATED BY
DELTA AIR LINES INC

DEPARTURE GATE E17 **SUBJECT TO CHANGE**

BAGS
01

Chapter 2

Beautiful in God's Sight

What does it mean to be beautiful?

I think we all know that women are supposed to believe that being beautiful isn't all about their physical appearance. "Be beautiful from the inside out," we're told. Sounds great! Let's do it! But what does it mean to be beautiful from the inside out? That doesn't really answer our original question. So let's define what a beautiful woman is: one who knows she is beautiful because of her Creator.

A beautiful woman lives a life with the fruit of the Spirit evident. Purpose is her best accessory. She wakes up each morning eager to serve, love, and be the person God created her to be.

I used to struggle with the desire to be "hot." I wanted guys to look at me and think, *Dang, she's beautiful.* Or even better, to say it out loud. I shared my thoughts with Jen, an older mentor, and told her the frustration I felt when I looked in the mirror.

You know what Jen did *not* do?

She did not correct me and say: "Grace, you are cute! Look at yourself!" She knew fake flattery would not satisfy my desire for physical approval.

She also did not respond with the typical girl-to-girl: "You're not ugly. In fact, just the other day, I heard so-and-so talking about how cute you are."

You know what Jen did?

She listened.

Months later, Jen and I traveled together to Kenya on a mission trip. One day in the city of Kiu, I was sitting with children all around me—tickling my sides, sitting on my lap, listening to me. I was sweaty. My clothes were modest. My hair was greasy and pulled in multiple directions.

I laughed as a little girl named Joy kept jumping into my lap. I pretended not to cry when the kids just about ripped off my scalp as they dug into my head to braid my hair. I was joyful, content, and loving life. In that moment, I did not care what any guy thought of me or what size bra I was wearing. All I cared about was the beautiful children surrounding me, and I was smiling because they were smiling.

Jen hadn't said anything when I'd shared my struggle with wanting to be hot, but I knew she'd heard me. And later that night she found the perfect time to reply: "I know you struggle with your beauty and worth, Grace. But you have never looked more beautiful than that moment when kids were surrounding you and you were simply loving them. That is beauty, and your ability to serve the Lord is your greatest purpose."

I will never forget those words.

Even now as I think about what Jen told me, I wonder what life would be like if we young women spent as much time encouraging one another as we do looking in the mirror. What if we spent as much time praying as we do covering our face with makeup? Yeah, I get that's the cheesy, classic Christian girl thing to say. But it's true. Notice I didn't say we should stop applying makeup. I am saying we shouldn't idolize the reflection in the mirror.

For Such a Time as This

Esther is one of my favorite Bible characters. She was a woman who found favor in the eyes of many—because she was beautiful—and she was chosen by King Ahasuerus to become his queen.

Meanwhile, Haman, one of the king's top officials, ordered a Jew named Mordecai to bow to him. Mordecai refused. Mordecai just happened to be Esther's cousin who had practically raised her. Haman was so mad at Mordecai that he convinced King Ahasuerus to kill every Jew within his empire. (Esther had not told the king that she was Jewish.)

Crazy story, right? It gets better.

Mordecai learned of the plot and sent a message to Esther, asking her to intercede with the king on the Jews' behalf. Except it wasn't so easy. By law, any man or woman who went to the king inside the inner court without being invited would be put to death.

Esther was understandably reluctant and sent word back to Mordecai of the situation. Here's part of Mordecai's response: "For if you keep silent at this time, relief and deliverance will rise for the Jews from another place, but you and your father's house will perish. And who knows whether you have not come to the kingdom for such a time as this?" (Esther 4:14, ESV).

Esther went to the king. And she survived. Through a series of God-ordained events, the king had Haman hanged on the very gallows he'd had built for Mordecai, he appointed Mordecai prime minister, and he issued a decree allowing the Jews to defend their lives whenever necessary.

Esther risked her life, and the Jews of Ahasuerus's kingdom were saved. She could have remained quiet, but she didn't. Why? Because Esther had a purpose.

There is one line in that last verse that I especially love: "for such a time as this."

Esther possessed beauty and royalty. But for such a time as this, there was something more important than keeping a hold on her crown and status.

Now, for you my friend, I believe that if God created you, He created you for big things. The same God that worked through Esther wants to use you for His purpose.

Here is what I think:

- *For such a time as this . . .* God created you to be something more beautiful than a pretty woman sitting on her throne—whatever you'd like your throne to be.
- *For such a time as this . . .* God created you to have something more important than a good-looking butt.
- *For such a time as this . . .* God created you for more than a pretty face in a selfie.
- *For such a time as this . . .* God created you for bigger purposes than just having guys think you're attractive.

Look in the Mirror

If you struggle with insecurity like I do, can I please ask you to go to your mirror? Yes, right now. Take the book with you.

Look into that mirror, and before you make any judgment about what you see looking back at you, boldly declare: "This woman is going to change the world. This woman is here right now for such a time as this."

Your purpose is not to look pretty. Your purpose is to make the world look more like God's kingdom each day. You should look like Christ, bearing fruit with every breath you take. You should be clothed with strength and dignity, showing joy in your not-so-great circumstances.

Pursue God, not compliments.

I'm not going to give you fake flattery. Instead, I will remind you of what makes a woman beautiful: it's knowing she is beautiful because of her Creator.

When we die and meet our Creator, He will not ask how many likes we got on our selfies or how many guys asked us out because we were hot. I can promise that whether guys thought we were beautiful will not even be a conversation. Instead, God will look at how we believed, loved, and lived.

God wants us to work daily to change the world, not our appearance.

Real Talk

- What is something radical you think God purposefully designed you for?
- What thought stood out most to you in this chapter? Why?
- Do you pursue God or compliments more?
- Write a prayer to God asking Him to remind you that He created you with a purpose for Him, not the world. Ask Him to use you for that purpose. And ask Him to point out the beauty that He sees in you.

LIE #2

Love must be earned.

Chapter 3

Love We Cannot Earn

There was a moment when I realized that my blog was becoming bigger than anything I imagined. As I sat, procrastinating writing a research paper for an upper-level journalism class, I stumbled upon a girl who wrote an open letter . . . about me . . . thanking me.

She simply thanked me for doing what I love—writing about our sweet Jesus. This girl was miles away at a university in California. I didn't know her, but I laughed because I once wrote an open letter to Taylor Swift. (So basically I'm Taylor Swift. Can I get in her squad now?)

However, just because a girl writes a complimentary open letter to you, that does not mean you are a "perfect Christian." I still fall into sin. I still find myself frustrated and feeling like I'm not living a life that deserves eternal love.

We've talked about resisting the world's definition of "good enough." But I'll admit that I still struggle with thinking I'm not good enough to be a Christian. Sometimes at church I don't feel

God at all during worship. I see everyone else's hands raised, and the thought hits me that they're good enough—but I'm not.

I'm far from the poster child of perfection. I've messed up a lot. I have too many regrets, mistakes, and sins to feel worthy of proclaiming myself a follower of the Savior who was beaten and crucified for the sake of proclaiming His love for me.

I doubt I'm the only one who feels that way.

My human instinct—and probably yours too—says I don't deserve to be forgiven or to be a Christian. I don't deserve to stand before God and hear, "Well done, good and faithful servant." My past makes me ashamed. My mistakes feel too dirty, too bad to be forgiven.

Get to Scraping

My freshman year of college, I went to fraternity parties and numbed my feeling of not being "cool enough" by drinking excessive amounts of alcohol. I thought alcohol was the only way I could be outgoing in social situations. No outgoing personality, no acceptance. No alcohol, no outgoing personality.

Well, after about fifteen shots at one party in particular, I woke up in my dorm room, a pink slip from the police next to my bed. It was a ticket for underage drinking. My RA had called the police after someone reported smelling alcohol on me.

I had been so drunk that I didn't remember taking the pink slip off my door when I returned home. Actually, I had been so drunk I didn't even remember returning home.

I felt as if God was talking to me through that pink slip: "You finished with this phase yet, Grace? You have some learning to do."

My punishment for the ticket was twelve hours of community service, a very difficult phone call to my very disappointed parents, and attendance at a class (complete with a research paper) on the dangers of alcohol. Thankfully, because it was my first offense, my record would be cleared upon completion. However, this all occurred right at the same time as finals.

I had heard that community service hours would be double-credited if I volunteered at a particular animal shelter from 7 to 9 a.m., so I signed up. I thought I'd found an easy way out—until I reported for duty and was handed a poop scraper from the owner of the shelter, whose less-than-happy demeanor made it seem like *she* was the one forced to do community service, not me.

"Get to scraping," she ordered.

Scraping poop gave me a lot of time to think. I wondered who had considered *white* tile for the landing spot of animal droppings a good idea. I wondered why God even created poop. I wondered why some people prefer small dogs over big dogs. (Come on: Golden Retrievers > Chihuahuas.)

I also thought about deeper matters. I thought about how I was broken and dirty, and that there was no way I was good enough for Christ. I considered myself too lost to be saved. After all, surely there was no way a perfect God with all the power in the universe would want to forgive a messed-up sinner like me. Was there?

I thought of that "good Christian girl" I knew. You know the type: that one girl who seems to have it all together at all times. She is perfect, always raising her hands when worship songs play. I bet she never spent her Wednesday mornings cleaning up animal droppings. She probably was still asleep, in her Pottery Barn room, with her Bible on her nightstand. Or already up, having a quiet time. *She never messes up*, I thought as I scraped my way along. *She is a better Christian than me. She is good enough for God's grace. But I'm not.*

At the shelter, I came to know a half-Basset Hound, half-some other undeterminable breed of dog. I called him Chester, and he was sweet and kind, albeit a little smelly. Each time I entered his station to clean up his poop, he watched me with those big ears framing his brown eyes. Then, as soon as I finished cleaning, he pooped. Every time. Like clockwork.

"Really, Chester?!?" I would yell at him when I knew no one could hear me. "When . . . will . . . you . . . learn?" (Trust me, the only thing more embarrassing than being the diligent college student cleaning up poop for community service is being the diligent college student cleaning up poop and trying to engage a dog in conversation.)

On my last day, I cleaned Chester's cage and he didn't poop after I finished. Miracle! I got the letter certifying my hours were served, and I said goodbye to Chester. I felt God tug on my heart as I petted Chester on top of the head.

"I clean up your mess," I sensed God saying. "One day you will become wiser."

God delivered a clear message through poop and a long-eared, smelly dog: God forgives me every day, but I still have the nerve to mess up what He has made clean. But guess what happens each time? Here comes God with His scraper, cleaning up behind me once more while still seeing my potential to increase in wisdom. I don't deserve that. I deserve to sit in my filth. But that is the cool thing about God. His love isn't for those who "deserve" Him. You can't earn His love. It is a gift, given to you for no other reason than He wants to give it to you.

Being a Christian

I've come to realize that being "good enough" isn't the point of being a Christian. Christianity isn't going down a checklist of things you must do to believe. A personal relationship with Christ is not about being the person with the flowing prayers at dinner, or the one who posts the most artsy photos with deep captions on social media. We shouldn't compare how we praise the Lord with how others praise Him. In fact, we should proclaim our love and belief in Christ differently, because we each have a unique relationship with Him.

Being a Christian is not a stroll through Central Park on a bright, shiny, seventy-degree day. It's not posting our coffee and Bible verse of the day while pretending our lives are perfect. It's not sitting in a pew for an hour on Sunday morning and thinking we've done what needs to be done to be spiritually prepared for the next week.

Christianity is rooted in Christ. It's a relationship with Him. It's about calling Him friend. It's about failing and admitting defeat. It's about knowing we're not perfect and that we're prone to wander. But it's also knowing that God gave His Son to die for our sins, and that we are forgiven by His grace alone—and definitely not by anything we've done.

Being a Christian means admitting that our poop stinks and that we mess up often. It means not forgetting that Jesus died for our sins two thousand years ago. It means being trained by the Holy Spirit and thanking the Creator for cleaning up the messes we make in our lives.

I used to strive to be the "perfect Christian." But as I continue to grow in relationship with Him, I continue to learn more about how not perfect I am. A perfect Christian is an oxymoron. Once you know God, you know His grace and your need for it every second.

We can't earn God's love. None of us deserve to call ourselves a friend of Christ. Since we're being honest here, He is way, way, way out of our league. But the beautiful thing about God's grace is that it's not fair. If grace was fair, we'd be in trouble. We don't deserve His forgiveness or a fifty-fourth chance at getting it right. Yet He continually is there, scraper in hand, and with a heart that loves us faithfully and consistently.

Ephesians 2:8–9 says, "For it is by grace you have been saved, through faith—and this is not from yourselves, it is the gift of God—not by works, so that no one can boast."

Being a Christian is not about raising your hands in church or the number of countries you have traveled to on mission trips. It's not about being perfect.

Being a Christian is not about hiding struggles. In fact, being a Christian is the opposite: it's admitting we struggle and confessing that because of God, and God alone, we are forgiven. We aren't forgiven because we've done a bunch of nice things, or because we've done more good than bad. We are forgiven because Christ died on the cross for our sins. We boast in His ability to love, not our ability to do good.

How do we know that we're Christians? Not by raising hands during worship, "giving up" our vacation time to serve overseas, or obtaining a seminary degree. We know we're Christians because we love God and do our best to worship Him through our daily actions.

Being a Christian is knowing you need a Savior and accepting His love while loving Him back.

Beyond Good Enough

The fact that He is so far out of our league makes what He did for us even sweeter.

We've earned nothing. Yet all that God asks of us is that we run to Him with all our flaws, with all our imperfections, with our worst mistakes, our addictions—yes, even our underage drinking tickets. When we run to Him, we will find freedom in Christ.

My friend, stop worrying about being good enough for Christ and simply admire His beauty. Admire His ability to clean up your mistakes, and thank Him that He does. God sees potential in you that you don't.

Once you've experienced this love, you'll want to be someone who shines His light and praises Him with your actions. I have learned that the devil's number one tactic for getting Christians to sin is to tell them, "God will forgive you—do it anyway!"

Too often, we take advantage of God's grace.

Too often, we take the cross lightly.

May I never take the cross lightly. God's sacrifice of sending His only Son to die a horrible death to cover the sins of all human-kind is a special gift. Jesus suffered physically and emotionally. As John 3:16 says, He did so out of love. For me. For you.

That's a love I want to say thank you for. That's a love I cannot go a day without admiring. That's a love that makes me want to love back by giving my own life as a sacrifice.

That's a love we couldn't earn.

Are you concerned that you'll mess up again? You will. We all will. But God cleans up our messes. Let us thank Him for giving up His Son's life, and three days later raising Him from the dead and emptying the tomb. Because that sacrifice has been made for us, let's give our best every day to bring Him glory.

If I had to earn God's love, I'd be in big-time trouble. But I can receive it, because He has given it to me freely. Let's let our lives serve as a dance that demonstrates His love so beautifully that others will want to join in.

Real Talk

- What can cause you to think you're not good enough for Christ?
- Does Christ call us to be "enough"?
- In what ways have you taken the cross lightly?
- Write a prayer of thankfulness to God for giving us a love we don't have to earn. List ways you can show your thankfulness.

Chapter 4

The Sex Chapter

I was twelve when I learned what purity meant. I took the pledge and asked my mom to buy me the cute "True Love Waits" purity ring all the girls at school had. Waiting until marriage to have sex seemed so easy back then. Even better, it was cool.

My friends and I sat in Sunday school promising we would wait until our wedding nights. Then we played M.A.S.H. and drew hearts around our crushes' names, only stopping our doodles to check on our Webkinz. Those were the easy days, right? Back when purity was cool, I didn't have crazy hormones, and even the Jonas Brothers had purity rings.

But then I grew up. And it became hard.

It starts with an innocent first crush, then a kiss. Then maybe you go a little bit further. But in society's view you're still a "virgin," so you are still doing what's right. *Right*?

Suddenly, you realize you are no longer the innocent girl repping her purity ring. Suddenly, you find yourself out on the town, looking for who you're going to kiss tonight. A kiss isn't bad, right?

Suddenly, you find yourself waking up in some guy's bed, texting your friends to come get you before he wakes up. Whether he's your boyfriend, the guy you are "talking" to, or someone you met on an app, you have that sinking feeling—shame. You know in your gut that although this is pleasing to the body, this is not who you want to be.

But everyone's doing it, so it's okay, right? Plus, that girl in your Bio class has sex way more than you ever have, so you're fine. Actually, you are a good girl compared to her. So it's okay. *Right?*

I'm going to be honest with you: I am technically a virgin. But that doesn't mean I've never struggled in the battle many face against sexual sin. In fact, I'm going to be real honest with you when I say I've been the girl who wakes up in bed with a boy, regretting my decision from the previous night. I've made mistakes that made me feel shameful.

I used to do what many of us women do: I created loopholes when discussing purity in my own life. I find this common in our generation. Maybe you have worked yourself into one of these loopholes involving purity:

- "I'm not having sex, so it's fine. The other stuff isn't actual sex."
- "I mean, we're going to get married. I think God meant sex is about being with the right person. So, it's okay to have sex if you are going to marry that person . . . eventually."
- "It's my body. I have the right to do what I want. Purity is an old-fashioned rule."
- "You don't wanna buy a car without a test drive. How would I know if I'm even attracted to my boyfriend if we don't have sex?"

Those are the lies we tell ourselves. But I want to talk about the truth.

1. Your body is not your own.

> Therefore, I urge you, brothers and sisters, in view of God's mercy, to offer your bodies as a living sacrifice, holy and pleasing to God—this is your true and proper worship. Do not conform to the pattern of this world, but be transformed by the renewing of your mind. Then you will be able to test and approve what God's will is—his good, pleasing and perfect will. (Romans 12:1–2)

Hear that? Your body is not your own.

I get it—you have "control." You have the free will to do with it what you please. But what if I told you that the most worthwhile action you can do with your body is to surrender it to God? Your actions should be given to Him. Your desires and temptations should be overruled. Obedience should take control of your body. Let this life and your actions be given back to the One who gave you life. His will is good. His will is pleasing. His will is perfect. If you are the only twenty-four-year-old virgin you know, that is okay. If you are the only person you know who went from having sex a lot to waiting for a man you haven't met, that is okay. And if your life looks different than everyone else's, that is okay too. In fact, it isn't just okay—it's great. God never called us to be like everyone else; He called us to be like our Savior.

In 1 Corinthians 6:19, the apostle Paul refers to our bodies as "temples of the Holy Spirit." Our bodies are meant to worship God. They were given to us for holy purposes. As a living sacrifice, your body is meant for more than hookups.

2. Purity comes from the heart and mind, not your body.

I used to think purity was all about being a virgin. However, once I began to dance with Jesus, I realized I had actually been struggling with purity in my past. I struggled with lust. I struggled with impure thoughts and a desire to stray. Even though I wasn't having "sex," I still was not living a pure life.

So how can we work on our purity? It starts with our hearts and our minds. It starts with our thoughts. Because our thoughts will soon become our actions.

In the Scripture passage we just discussed, it talks about being transformed by the renewing of your mind. In previous sex talks, I always got the classic lines: "Don't watch those bad movies, and don't close the door when hanging with a boy." Those are good steps. However, that doesn't stop the problem of lust. And yes, girls lust.

It starts with your thoughts: "Finally, brothers and sisters, whatever is true, whatever is noble, whatever is right, whatever is pure, whatever is lovely, whatever is admirable—if anything is excellent or praiseworthy—think about such things" (Philippians 4:8).

Pray for thoughts like these. Strive to wake up each morning and live out these thoughts. Surround yourself with people who are trying to think on these things as well. Is that party Friday night really going to help you think pure and lovely thoughts? Is alcohol going to allow you to think about what is admirable?

Your actions are a reflection of your thoughts. Strive to think about whatever is true, noble, right, pure, lovely, admirable, excellent, and praiseworthy.

3. Sex is awesome!

Or so I've been told. I am excited to have sex for the first time on my wedding night, and I'm super excited that my first time will be with my husband. Sex is a wonderful act, but it's one that God created to be enjoyed only within marriage as He defined it.

Our bodies crave sex before marriage because God gave us emotions and hormones that cause us to want to have sex. Yes, God gave us sex as the means for reproduction—it's how He creates His favorite creation. But it's also a gift from God for enjoying an intimate connection with our spouses. He designed our bodies for sex, which is a beautiful expression of love between two people who honor Him with their bodies.

I have noticed that we twentysomethings can try to mix God's will with our will. So maybe we wait for the "right" person instead of waiting until we are married. Or until after college instead of marriage.

We create loopholes.

We say, "Well, God didn't mean it like *that*." Actually, He did. He meant it exactly like that. Stop searching for loopholes and focus on trusting His good, perfect, and pleasing will. Remember it is God's will, not our will.

4. Purity is not only about sex before marriage.

To the wife thinking, "This chapter isn't for me—I'm already married," please know I thought of you, too, as I wrote this material.

Purity is about doing your best to stay away from the wicked ways of the world. It's about maintaining pure thoughts about your neighbor, respecting the coworker who sometimes annoys you, and making sure that what you watch, eat, and do in your spare time pleases God.

Something as simple as watching a movie that causes your thoughts to become sinful is not striving for purity.

Being pure means going against the world's patterns and

seeking to have your mind filled with thoughts that build God's kingdom. That doesn't come easy, and I would say in order to have the fruit of purity in your life, you need to plant yourself near like-minded people—people who have already harvested that fruit. You need community and accountability in order to create pure and pleasing thoughts.

Here's something else to keep in mind: We single ladies need wisdom from married women. Christians need to talk more about sex, and we need you to be part of those conversations, whether you are starting them or joining them. So keep reading!

Accountability not only helps us with our behavior, but even confessing and repenting of our sinful thoughts out loud lightens the load of shame and darkness we carry inside, where the enemy has his strongest hold. God never ever called us to go through this life alone. He has not only given us Himself, He gave us each other to be mirrors of Him for our community.

5. God's boundaries for sex are good for you.

Some of you may have an experience like this in your memory bank: You were four or five years old, chilling in the kitchen while your mom cooked mac and cheese. As you impatiently waited for the mac and cheese, the stove looked interesting to you. Your mom said something like, "Do not touch the stove." That made the stove even more tempting. Your curiosity trumped her wisdom, and you touched the stove. If that's you, your mom knew what she was talking about, didn't she?

God knows what He's talking about, too, when it comes to the boundaries He placed around sex. He's not trying to keep you from having fun. Instead, He knows you'll enjoy sex (and all that goes with it) more if you follow His plan.

Sex instantly changes a relationship. I think that's even truer for young women. No matter how chill you are, you are giving away your emotions each time you have sex—and I'm not talking only about intercourse, ladies.

I've seen friends wake up in the morning and deal with the regret and pain of realizing they gave it all to a guy the night before. I've heard their heartaches. I've watched them spiral into an irreversible cycle when they decide, "We've had sex once, so why not again?"

As the designer of sex, God knows exactly what needs to be in the instruction manual. When He says wait until marriage, He knows what He is talking about. I've committed to enjoy sex the way God created it to be. And that means waiting until marriage.

6. Being pure shows obedience to God. It also gives you the opportunity to share a special bond with your future husband.

At sixteen, I experienced my first kiss. (Wonder if he knows I'm writing a book now?) I started a prayer journal for my future husband that night. I have clear memories of a crush and the butterflies that accompanied it, but I also remember sensing that the cute baseball star with the brown hair was not my future husband.

That night, I wrote in my journal:

Dear Future Husband,

So, this journal will be for you, whoever you are. I pray for your first kiss and for your butterflies. I pray for whatever you are going through and that when we meet, you will be the man I need. And I know that these boys are only temporary—they're

33

not you, and I will not go further with any boy who isn't you.
I'm praying for you from now until we die.

XOXO

Your Wife

I kept the prayer journal a secret until college. When I've trusted someone enough to tell them of its existence, reactions typically go one of two ways:

1. "Awwwh, that's cute!"
2. "Are you serious?" accompanied by a smirk and sarcastic laugh.

The second doesn't bother me. I'm proud of the journal. Besides, it's for my future husband, not them.

I pray for my husband a lot, and some people think that's cheesy too. But the journal has stopped me from dating guys who I knew deep down would never be the man to read my letters.
I think my future husband will think my journal is kinda sexy!

Journaling might be a good way for you to think about your future husband—and to remind yourself that your virginity is a beautiful gift to him. Perhaps that will help you resist the temptations you face. A journal also can serve as a great reminder to pray for your future husband.

7. If you've had sex, don't think, "Too late."

I realize that a good number of you have read this chapter thinking, "Well, it's too late for me on this one."

I disagree.

You'll never find a place in the Bible where it was too late for someone's sins to be forgiven; you'll never find a person whose sins were too bad for Jesus to forgive. The Bible is a collection of people's stories about messing up, seeing the light, and changing for the better. That can be you, and that can apply to sex.

I have a wonderful friend who did not wait to have sex until marriage. She was in a relationship with a guy, and sex had become part of that relationship. She realized the Lord was calling her to stop her impurity. It was difficult, and she and her boyfriend eventually broke up.

My friend talks about the moment she attended the wedding of a friend who was marrying a guy she met at church. Those two didn't have sex before marriage, which wasn't a surprise to anyone who knew them. Their relationship was centered on Jesus. During the ceremony, as my friend reflected on the bride and groom's relationship, she began feeling dirty. She could feel people looking at her and thinking, *Yep, the girl in the fourth row has had sex— multiple times.*

My friend thought in that moment: *I will never find a love like that. I will have to marry a guy who isn't a virgin—like me.*

Wrong! No! Many times, no!

That is not how the gospel works. God doesn't say, "Although I have made you 'new,' you don't deserve a virgin since you're not one yourself. It's too late for that. Sorry."

God's grace doesn't work that way.

Because of grace, even though you may not physically be a virgin, you can still be clean. You can stop having sex and commit to not having sex again until you're married, and then you and your husband will both appreciate that you did something to be proud of with the fresh start God gave you. I know virgins and non-virgins who have married, and I've noticed there is a special kind of love and understanding on the virgin's part when they realize their partner made a lifestyle change and held that commitment into marriage. That actually makes for a pretty good love story.

Let me be clear about this: if the person you are planning on marrying has not forgiven you for your past mistakes, run. I don't care if he goes to church every Sunday. If a man doesn't see that your past is a testament to God's grace, then he isn't loving you as your Savior does.

You are not an "unwrapped" present. There's nothing I dislike more than when Christians give the "sex talk" and use that metaphor. The Lord cherishes each of us. We are all worthy presents. Any guy who thinks you are an unwrapped present because of your past needs to be reminded of what Jesus did on the cross. We are all presents, beautiful presents, worthy of a love that is a reflection of the Savior's love.

Do you see the value in yourself? Do you recognize that you, my friend, are a gift?

We live in a world of hookups. But you can choose to be different, as God has called you to be. A body that has engaged in activities that dishonored God can become a body that honors God. If you've had sex, regardless of how many times and with how many guys, it's not too late to say you're done with sex until marriage. Even if you're in a relationship with your future husband, honor God in your relationship and watch how He honors your relationship in return.

You are beautiful, and the man standing there as you make your way down the aisle will be one lucky dude. Wait for him. Make that promise.

Aren't you glad we had this talk?

Real Talk

- Do you struggle with the idea of waiting for marriage to have sex?
- Do you ever search for loopholes? If yes, what loophole?
- Which of these six truths spoke the most to you? Why?
- Other than sex, what is an area of your life that isn't pure?
- What goal do you need to set for yourself after reading this chapter?

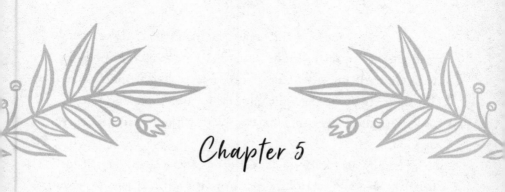

Chapter 5

Finding a Guy Who Doesn't Wait Because of You

*W*hoa, Grace. What's up with that chapter title? Didn't you just spend a chapter talking about waiting for my future husband? I'm confused!"

Let me clear that up for you. But first, a story.

I was working at a summer camp in the mountains of North Carolina. I grew up going to this camp and worked on staff there during the summers after my senior year in high school until my sophomore year of college. One year, I was a counselor for high school girls, which meant I got to have a bunch of dance parties, deep talks, and sleepovers with girls who were cooler than me. One conversation from that camp still stands out, because although the girl was sixteen, she was dealing with a common problem for Christian women of all ages.

The camper and I were sitting criss-cross applesauce on the front porch of our cabin when she began telling me about "the guy."

He was a good guy and smart. He bought her flowers and made her feel special. But he didn't have much of a relationship with God. He knew God on a surface level, but he didn't show any desire to go deeper. The guy was focused more on football, partying, and pretending he was okay without daily reliance on God.

The guy also knew my sweet camper was saving herself for marriage. He said he didn't need to wait until marriage to have sex but that he would wait for her. My camper thought that was romantic of him.

I could have told a similar story to hers not much earlier. I'd had a relationship with a guy who was great in some respects. I was focused on my boyfriend's body, looks, and good-guy characteristics. When he said he would wait to have sex because of me, I thought that was sweet. It sounded like a Hollywood movie in the making—a really good guy with just enough "bad boy" in him for other girls to envy me, and he was putting aside his wishes and waiting because of his Christian girlfriend.

Perfect, right?

Except, that script fell apart for me.

He couldn't wait after all, and during spring break he found someone who would have sex with him. I found out the next day when a girl who had previously dated him publicly confronted me and, with spite in her voice, announced that he had hooked up with someone else.

My tears were more than a cry of betrayal. I was heartbroken that some random girl had given the guy one thing I would never give him. Our relationship didn't end well.

So with the benefit of experience, I looked in my camper's eyes and said: "If he doesn't love the Author of love, how can he love you? If he's waiting because of you—not because of what God instructed regarding sex—then is he really making a wise choice?"

Relationships can be tricky, and hormones are always confusing. If you decide to invest in a relationship with someone who is not pursing God, then their idea of love probably differs from yours.

If he isn't following Who he should be following, he could lead you astray. He is honoring your beliefs, not his own. Honestly, how long do you think that will last? Especially with an act that carries as much temptation and peer pressure as sex?

Let me be clear: waiting until marriage to have sex is admirable. It's being obedient to God. Finding a guy who says he will wait for marriage is wonderful. But he shouldn't make that commitment to please you. His purpose should not be to be a good boyfriend. He should wait because he wants to please God. He should wait because he knows his body is a living sacrifice, created to honor and praise the Savior who died for his sins.

My desire is no longer "finding the right guy." I want to find God. I want to know more about His character. I want to focus on putting Him first, not some guy. I believe that as I pursue God, I will meet a man who is pursuing Him, too, and our two pursuits will become one.

May I suggest three relationship goals for you?

1. Wait for a man who waits because of God, not because of you.
2. Wait for a man who puts Jesus first, not you.
3. Wait for a man who is in love with Jesus, his first love, more than he is in love with you.

So, yes, look for someone who holds the door open, buys you a meal, and asks about your day. Find someone who makes you blush when he compliments you, who cares for you, and who treats you special. But most of all, pray for someone who seeks Christ's approval above yours.

I mess up. I am sinful. I fail. I don't want a man who thinks I can be his foundation. I'd hope you don't, either.

You'll have a much better chance of finding a man who pleases you if you start with finding a man who first pleases God.

Real Talk

- Have you desired a guy who waited only "for you"?
- What attracts us to a good guy who has a little bit of "bad boy" in him?
- What would it look like to have a relationship with a guy whose first aim is to please God?
- Pray to have your priorities properly aligned: you seeking God first and a relationship with a guy who also seeks Him first.

Chapter 6

The Best Love Story Ever

Everybody has a story, the saying goes. I believe that's true. But there are some people who *really* have a story.

You know who I'm talking about here—those with incredible stories about who they were before they knew Jesus. Horrible things happened to them, their lives got flipped upside down and then—BAM!—there Jesus was, clear as can be, speaking to them through a modern-day version of a burning bush.

I'm thinking of the alcoholic sex addict whose soul was all but lost until he found Jesus. Or the woman who was happy in a life filled with material possessions, not thinking she needed anything else, much less Jesus, until she lost everything. Then she discovered Jesus had been there all along, waiting for her to realize He was the only thing in life she truly needed. I've heard and read of people who claimed to hear God's voice or to unmistakably see Him in a dream or vision.

Those are the types of stories that leave me asking, "When is *that* movie coming out?"

Yet at the same time, I'm asking myself, "Why haven't I had a crazy-cool Jesus moment?" Or "Why does God speak so clearly to this guy and give him an inspiring story, while I'm over here feeling nothing?" Or "Why does God 'show up' differently for her than He does for me?"

I've even wondered why I get jealous of someone for having a more eventful and, sometimes, more painful life than me. I've actually caught myself thinking, *It would be worth enduring that pain for that story.*

The truth is, when I measure my story against the stories of others, mine loses most of the time. The other person's story is almost always cooler. It brings everyone in the room to tears. I don't dare follow with mine.

Given that, I got scared when I decided to write a book. I have the blogging thing down. I'm good with that. But a *book?* Books are for those with unbelievably incredible stories. You know, those who died and saw heaven. Or won a gold medal (or two or three) in the Olympics. Or went to jail and accepted Jesus after reading one of the Bibles given to prisoners by some awesome ministry. Or starred on a reality show and stuck to their beliefs even amid the pressure and temptations of Hollywood.

I love those stories. But none of those are the stories of an ordinary recent college graduate like me.

Sure, I've had my heart broken. A few times, in fact. I've lost loved ones. I've gone through some stuff. But to me, my story just seems too common for other people to find interesting.

How can God, I've wondered, *use my ordinary life to show people how extraordinary His love is?*

But then, somewhere early in my writing process, I recalled a conversation I'd had with a camper at summer camp. The girl woke me up in the middle of the night to tell me she was jealous of another camper whose story had made our whole cabin cry. She didn't think her own story—having her heart broken by a guy—was worthy of sharing with the other girls. She wanted to experience God in a deep way like the other camper had.

"I know how you feel," I said, both of us in tears.

"But one day," I continued, "God is going to use that heartbreak you think isn't important enough to share, and through that experience you are going to help grow His kingdom. Just because your story is different than hers doesn't mean it can't help someone else see God's glory."

Then I shared my one small heartbreak story with her. Because of my experience, I was able to describe the pain I'd felt and how I had learned that when God's children cry, He cares and wants to comfort us. God doesn't think our problems are too small. He invites us to come to Him as we are and to talk with Him. When we do, He's able to ease our pains and mend our broken hearts. He wants to do that for us, because we are His creation. He loves us. Not because of anything we have done, not because we've earned it or deserve it, but simply because we are His.

The dangerous game of comparison is not only for looks, money, and possessions. It's also way too easy to compare our faith and our relationships with Christ to those around us. That is a game we're not set up to win.

Trust me: as many times as I've played that game, I know we can't win.

God works in different people's lives in different ways. The way He speaks into your life will be different than how He speaks into the life of the person next to you. It's crazy to think that the Creator of everything is so into us as individuals that He speaks to each of us personally. No one-size-fits-all communication from God!

He's that real, He's that into you, and *He* is the author of your story. So trust Him. Don't worry about how your story measures up against anyone else's. Stop playing that game. Instead, just listen and rejoice over how God is working in the lives of those around you.

And don't fall into the trap of thinking your story isn't good enough.

We can think that love has to be packaged, delivered, and expressed a certain way. As if we have to earn God's love through a remarkable story—by building an orphanage in Africa, attending rehab, or becoming a motivational speaker. But that's not the case.

God gave you the life you're living to be a story that brings glory to Him. It's essential to remember that *He* is your life. Your value comes from your faith in Him. The story of your faith should spread His name, not yours.

If your story causes people to cry and see Jesus, great. Share it! If you think your story is too ordinary, share it anyway! You might be surprised at who it could point to Jesus. Embrace your story—whatever it is. He's written it just for you.

Ultimately, we all share one key element in our stories as followers of Christ: Jesus died on a cross and conquered the grave so that we can spend eternity with Him in heaven. If you ask me, *that* is an incredibly unbelievable story that we didn't earn, but were given.

Share it!

Real Talk

- What is your story?
- How can God use your story for His kingdom?
- Is there a time that you felt jealous because someone else's story was better? Put the jealousy aside and think about what you like about her story. What can you learn about God from her story?
- Pray and thank God for the story He has given you. Ask for boldness and courage to share it with others. You may not believe this, but there's someone out there who needs to hear *your* story.

LIE #3

Forget your past.

Chapter 7

When Your Smile Is Broken

Visualize this: It's seventh grade picture day. You've managed to place yourself in four clubs, so there will be plenty of photos to pose for. You wear your favorite Aeropostale shirt. Suddenly, as you slip the silly bands onto your wrist and over-fry your side bangs, you see it in the mirror.

Only half of your face is working.

You smile, and only half of your face lifts. You try to blink, and only one eye winks. You raise your eyebrows, and only half of your forehead wrinkles. One side of an imaginary line right down the middle of your face is doing what your brain is telling it to do. The other half of your face decided not to report for work today.

Your smile is broken.

That happened to me. At age twelve, I came down with Bell's palsy, a condition in which the muscles on one side of the face become paralyzed or barely move. That side of the face droops while the other carries on as normal. The exact cause is unknown, although it can be a reaction to a viral infection. Most often, the symptoms are temporary and are gone within six weeks.

In the long run, Bell's palsy usually isn't a big deal. When it shows up on picture day, it's a major problem. I can laugh about my pictures now, but the concept of a broken smile has remained with me since.

Broken Smiles

My experience with Bell's palsy was my first broken smile, but it wasn't the last. Not by a long shot. You see, during middle school I pretty much hated my life. It started when a group of boys told me I'd never have a boyfriend. Every day they'd say I was ugly and "joke" that my forehead was so big it could be a runway.

Finally, on the last day of eighth grade, I cried in front of those bullies. For the first time they realized that, despite the fake smiles I'd always forced when they teased me, I was actually hurting— and hurting bad. They finally saw my broken smile.

I was pretending to be happy. Half of me got it right. Half of me smiled through the day, ignored the insults, and went along pretending I was fine. But I was not fine.

That afternoon, I remembered that you could die by closing the garage door and turning on the car. I slipped into the driver's seat and, with tear-filled eyes, prepared to insert the key into the ignition and end my life. If I was ugly and everyone hated me, why was life worth living?

But before I started the car, I felt God's presence in a way I had never experienced. It was as if He whispered into my heart: "Grace, you will use this pain one day. I make all things work together for good. And My good *is* good." So, I put the keys away and went back inside to bed.

The dangers of bullying receive more attention now than they did then, but I still hear from those who think it's odd that middle school bullying could drive someone to consider suicide. I'm proof it's true. And very real. In fact, the bullying I experienced from almost a decade ago still negatively affects me. The insecurities that developed then haunt me on days when I don't feel pretty or wonder why I'm single. But in those moments, God has consistently reminded me that He considers me worthy and that He is my source of joy.

That second broken smile—not the temporary one from Bell's palsy—started in middle school as the girl who put on a happy face to hide the pain of the jokes but secretly cried every day. A few years later, in high school, that formerly bullied girl was voted onto the homecoming court and selected as class president. You might think those accomplishments made everything okay again. But I was secretly fighting a losing battle with an eating disorder.

Like my smile on picture day, my life was broken. I was a pro at pretending to be happy. Most of my friends had no idea what I was going through. I looked and acted happy, but behind my locked bedroom door, my fake smile gave way to real tears. I was hopeless.

The girl who was "fine" soon realized she wasn't. We so often hide half of our emotions, feelings, and struggles from the world. Our generation has become great actors and actresses. On social media, we act like the breakup isn't phasing us, that we *just love* the new city our job is in, and that our family never has problems. But then we crack. The "fine" side gets tired of holding it all together. And in those moments, we realize our smile was broken the whole time.

Inside the closed garage, I was ready to stop pretending. As I contemplated my purpose and could not come up with one reason to live, God gave me one: Himself.

The only constant we have is God. And through Him we are given hope and joy.

Smiles of Joy

I don't see a lot of consistency in this world. Some days we're cool; others we're lame. Some days we are eating a juicy steak, others are the fifth consecutive meal of Ramen noodles. Sometimes we bite into a chocolate chip cookie only to taste oatmeal raisin. Circumstances can bring temporary happiness just as well as they can cause sadness.

Life can stink sometimes, but we can find rest despite its inconsistency because we worship a God who consistently loves us. If He can hold the whole world in His hands, then surely He can give us joy when life stinks, can't He?

There was a woman who experienced that firsthand in the Bible. She was a Samaritan woman who had committed many sexual sins.

Jesus was sitting alone by a well when this woman approached. It was about noon, the hottest part of the day, which was a weird time to haul around a big jug of water in the desert. But the woman chose that time so she could avoid people who would shame her. Going against social customs, Jesus, who was a Jew, approached the Samaritan woman and asked for a drink. That started a conversation, and Jesus told the woman living in sin about a different type of water that could satisfy her.

Jesus answered, "Everyone who drinks this water will be thirsty again, but whoever drinks the water I give them will never thirst. Indeed, the water I give them will become in them a spring of water welling up to eternal life." (John 4:13–14)

I recommend reading that whole chapter so you can hear the rest of the story. But in short, Jesus called the woman out for having many men in her life. But he didn't stop there, as everyone else who knew her reputation presumably had, He offered her living water that could quench any desire she had.

She accepted.

The Samaritan woman had been living with a broken smile. She felt so scorned by society that she had gone to the well at the safest time to avoid being seen. She was confused that a Jew would talk to her. She had been finding her value in men who couldn't satisfy her. Although she may have appeared okay, she was filling her life with the wrong things of the world. She was dying.

Then one unplanned conversation with Jesus changed her eternity. She realized she was talking with the Messiah, so she hurried off to tell the people of her town—those same people she'd been avoiding. Verse 39 says, "Many of the Samaritans from that town believed in [Jesus]"—get this!—"*because of the woman's testimony*" (emphasis mine).

The woman with the broken smile didn't just leave happy—she left joyful because she found in that living water the satisfaction she'd been longing for. Jesus placed a full smile in her life.

Perhaps you are searching for happiness when you should be seeking joy. You won't find it in acceptance from the cool people at work. You won't find it in how many guys like your posts. If those pursuits become the well you drink from, you'll wind up with a broken smile. Only Christ offers what can truly satisfy you. Only He can give you joy.

Life isn't always easy, but please remember that you are here for a reason. Your life is no mistake, and God is ready to turn your trial into a testimony. If you ever feel like you are living a broken-smile life, please tell someone. Talk to a counselor, pastor, family member, or loved one. Also, talk to Jesus. Pray for joy. Pray for more of Him. Accept His love and never be thirsty again.

Stop hiding behind the "I'm fine" lie. Start accepting that you aren't fine. And feel. Be sad. Talk to a friend. Start accepting that your trial is hard and you need Jesus on your team. Start accepting your need for Him. Because when you see your need for God, you begin to see the world's need for you. The world needs you to take up your cross and show His love. The world needs you to show them what a life filled with joy is like.

There's nothing like a smile produced by joy. I just wish I'd had one on picture day.

Real Talk

- Do you find yourself, like the Samaritan woman, filling your life with things that cannot fully satisfy you?
- What actually can satisfy you?
- How can you allow yourself to consume the living waters that satisfy?
- Pray that the Holy Spirit will remind you of who can satisfy you, and of what will come up short.

Chapter 8

Through Jesus' Eyes

Trevor (not his real name) was one of the middle-school boys who bullied me by making fun of my forehead and saying I was so ugly I'd never have a boyfriend. During high school, Trevor became a Christian.

He didn't just become a Christian, though. He became an all-in, pedal-to-the-metal, sold-out Christian.

Trevor immediately got active in all the Christian clubs at school. He started asking classmates to go to church. He was almost pushy in trying to get other students to come to a relationship with Jesus.

I didn't like Trevor being a Christian. His words had haunted me all those years. The first time I read a social media post where he posted a Bible verse, my mind went into overdrive.

Couldn't he just pick another religion? Can't he get involved in a sport or something else instead? Seriously, Trevor? Wouldn't you rather go back to not being a Christian? You were mean before. Stay mean. Christianity is my thing!

Basically, my thoughts settled on this one major idea: *Trevor does not deserve to have Christ in his heart until he tells me he's sorry for what he did to me.*

Not the most angelic of thoughts, for sure. The angels may rejoice when a sinner repents, but I sure didn't with Trevor. I kept my anger inside, but it would boil up to the top again whenever I'd see pictures of him on Instagram being active in *my* religion.

With time, I like to think that Trevor and I kind of became friends. But I never really forgave him for the mean things he'd said about me. His and his friends' words ate away at me every day. They spoke lies so often that I started to believe them as truth. My perception of worth assigned by their words led to suicidal thoughts and actions. I almost killed myself because of how he and the other guys had teased me. So, the fact that he talked about his faith really frustrated me. He even went on mission trips and served *my* God. How painful!

It took about three years and a trip to the gym to realize how wrong those thoughts were.

No More Better-Thans

My junior year in college, my headphones weren't working when I stepped onto my frenemy, the StairMaster. I set the timer for thirty minutes and decided that without Pandora, I'd just have to pass the time contemplating my decision to work out.

Two bubbly, high-ponytailed women took up spots on the StairMasters next to me. They began to talk, and my nosy self couldn't help but listen. I mean, what's a girl to do when she can't listen to songs about exes?

The women's conversation started something like this:

"Oh my goodness. So, Amanda got so drunk that she hooked up with Brad. And *then* she had the nerve to show up at church the next day. Ha-ha. Nice try! You're not fooling anyone."

Oh. My bad. Did I miss someplace where Jesus said, "Hey, before you enter my place of worship, make sure you don't hook up with anyone"?

Yeah, I don't think that's in the Scriptures.

The conversation got worse.

"Like, Amanda is not fooling anyone with this wannabe Christian act. She is def not a Christian. And to make it worse, she legit still had the X's on her hand at church."

I must have missed that part too. Apparently, wearing an X from being underage in a bar is a disqualifier from needing Jesus. Perhaps the eleventh commandment was, "Thou shalt not try to have a relationship with Me if thou hast Xs on thy hands from thy bar." I must pay more attention when I read the Bible!

All right, friends. Let's get this straight. None of us is better than the girl who hooked up with the drunk boy last night, or the girl who threw up at the bar. We are not better than the girl who got slapped with a minor in consumption, or the boy who cheated on his girlfriend. I'm not better. You're not better. We're all sinners.

I've been both the girl being judged for her actions and the girl doing the judging. It hurts in both directions. But I also have been the once-messed-up-sinner running into Jesus' arms on the heels of my sins.

We all have to start somewhere. Just because someone is lost doesn't mean she won't eventually wind up in the right place. If you are a believer, you just made it to the right place sooner than the person you're judging. That's true for me, and I know all about being lost.

I get lost in the grocery store. I've bought bagels at least 293 times, yet I still have to ask sweet Susan the H-E-B employee how to find the carb aisle. But I always manage to get back on track and grab my bagels—*and* stop by the ice cream aisle for some Ben and Jerry's. Talk about success!

I rely on my phone map to drive to my favorite restaurant. I know that's pathetic, but here's my point: it's easy to get off the intended path—even when we *should* know the way. When it happens, we need to admit we've strayed and be pointed back in the right direction.

In spiritual terms, we're all sinners in desperate need of a Savior. We all must confess our sins and focus on answering God's big question: "Will you follow Me?"

Getting off that StairMaster, I felt the temptation to believe my sins were different than Amanda's. But the truth is, they weren't. They were dirty, they were manipulative, and they separated me from God.

When I was the one acting out and being judged, I was sinning. I was prideful. And my sins were just as dirty as Amanda's sins. My pride prohibited me from seeing how beautiful God's grace was for a messed-up, frequent sinner like me.

I also have been like those women on the StairMasters, which takes me back to Trevor.

I spent years angry with Trevor because he chose to become a Christian. He hurt me, and because of that, I reasoned, he did not deserve Christ. I didn't like the person Trevor used to be. I hadn't forgiven him. I didn't believe he was sorry. The pain of his words still crushed me at times.

It wasn't until during my senior year that I casually brought up the bullying to Trevor and laughed it off. I wanted to see his reaction, especially whether or not he felt guilty.

"Grace, seriously, give me a hug," he said. "I feel bad about those days a lot, and I truly am sorry."

I thanked him and I went into the bathroom to cry. I had to decide to actually forgive him, to let go of my resentment toward him. In that moment, I did. My only regret is not forgiving him earlier, because although grace feels great to receive, it feels even better to give.

Here's an important truth: as the body of believers, we need to celebrate brothers and sisters who come to know Christ. We need to celebrate that their "used to's" are "no more's." "Used to's" are God at work, making people new through grace when they follow Him. God gives that grace to all, including me, you, and even Trevor (or anyone who has previously hurt you).

So, if the girl sitting next to you at church hooked up with someone the night before—welcome her. What a great day for her to decide to attend church! Don't gossip about her "used to's" at the gym.

If a guy who used to be mean to you walks through your church doors—do something unexpected and hug him. Forgive him before he apologizes. Forgive him even if he doesn't apologize. I know that doesn't sound fun or easy, and I know I didn't do that with Trevor at first. But I wish I had. Besides, God forgave us, didn't He?

Real Church

Let's be real: the church has some problems that shouldn't be problems. I've heard of church splits occurring over the color of new carpet. I've heard of people griping at the pastor because it was too cold in the sanctuary—the same sanctuary that some thought was too hot. Just about the only thing I haven't heard yet is a church that lost people because the doughnuts were from Walmart instead of Krispy Kreme. (If that has happened at your church, please let me know. I must hear the full story.) But real problems grow in churches where people treat it like an exclusive country club. Or a place to gossip about so-and-so's latest mistake.

A church is supposed to be a welcoming and accepting body of believers who strive to maintain a place where others can feel wanted, cared for, and—as the Holy Spirit sees fit—convicted of their sins.

Shouldn't we be worried about condoning sinful behavior? That's a common thought in church circles. But choosing to welcome Amanda and those like her to church—to make her feel accepted—does not mean it was right for her to hook up with Brad. Far from it. Scripture makes that clear.

What I am saying is that we are not the judge. God is. And we need to have the types of churches where the Holy Spirit convicts people of their sins and gives them a fresh start. That's *His* role. Our calling as a body of believers is to be such encouraging hosts to the Amandas out there that they see our relationships with Christ and want one too.

When necessary, as friends and a church community, we can help our brothers and sisters learn the truth about sin and remind them of the life God calls each of us to live. But first, ask yourself three good questions as a check of your intentions, heart, and relationship:

1. Is your intent to make yourself look good or to help your brother or sister seek truth?
2. Are you trying to gain anything for yourself, such as compliments, status, or favors? Or are you sincerely striving to direct your friend closer to the Savior?
3. Do you have a close enough relationship with this person? Jesus knew people's stories and the truth about their lives before confronting them. Do you know the truth about this person, or are you working off gossip? Have you strived to get to know her heart before striving to change her heart?

When it comes to being a disciple of Jesus, I've learned that I will mess up. Although I'm trying to grow in obedience to Him, I'm not perfect. When I fall, I get back up and onto the right path—hopefully a little wiser and stronger because of the experience. I have sins that I've struggled with, but I've made it a priority to be in the church pew the next Sunday. It's not that the act of going to church redeems me; it's the truth of the gospel I hear as I'm surrounded by a healthy community. I serve a God who sees my imperfections and doesn't need to ask what I've done the week before. He already knows. And He wants to communicate with us about our downfalls.

God doesn't ask us to wash the Xs off our hands. He says, "Come as you are." He welcomes us to His table. He doesn't ask Amanda to pretend she never looked at Brad. He asks her to turn to Him, learn from her mistake, and follow Him. Seriously, if God welcomes Amanda into His house the morning after she hooked up with Brad, shouldn't we welcome her too? It's *His* house!

We serve a loving and forgiving God who challenges us to live holy lives. When we ask forgiveness for our sins, He asks, "What will you do?" instead of "What did you do?" The fancy word for this is *sanctification*—the process of daily refining our fallen habits.

If you feel weighed down by your sins, throw off the weight. Look to the cross. A perfect, blameless man with no sins of His own carried *your* sins to *His* cross. No sin, no amount of sins, were too much for him to carry.

If you think you're great and don't need His help, I pray you'll see the error of that thinking. You need His love. You need His grace. And you need to answer that question He's whispering into your heart: "Will you follow Me?"

When you decide to follow Him, ask Him to help you love like Him. Ask Him to help see people the way He sees them. That will change your perspective, for sure. Learn to view people through this undeserved lens, and you'll welcome Amanda instead of belittling her. In time, you'll forgive Trevor, celebrate that he decided to become your brother in Christ, and pray for him as he progresses on his Christian journey. You'll look beyond her Xs and his mean words. And most important, you will care for and support them.

That's what is supposed to happen in a church. Brokenness is welcomed. Forgiveness is granted. Christ's love is celebrated.

Do you help promote that atmosphere in your church?

As James 4:12 says, "There is only one Lawgiver and Judge, the one who is able to save and destroy."

Judging is for God.

Real Talk

- Have you judged someone for their sins?
- What do you think motivated you to judge them?
- What should you have done instead of judging them?
- Pray for understanding, empathy, and a heart that loves your brothers and sisters in Christ rather than having an attitude that judges them for their words and actions.

LIE #4

When you don't look
"presentable," hide.

Chapter 9

Get Out from Under That Cap

*I*sat in a coffee shop on a Friday afternoon, journal open in front of me, chin tucked and hat pulled down to avoid making eye contact with anyone.

When I looked into the mirror that morning, my face resembled a pepperoni pizza.

Really?!? I thought acne went away when you graduated high school. Or at least when you reached your twenties.

Nope, at least not for me. As if the acne wasn't bad enough, my hair had been unusually stubborn that morning. I hopelessly surrendered to throwing my hair into a messy bun and grabbing my go-to "my hair hates me today" hat.

And so there I sat, hiding in the coffee shop, hoping that finding a deep thought or two for my journal would help me unwind from a long week. At least it was Friday—I could celebrate that. My only concern for the next two days was what to watch on Netflix.

Then I saw him—a really good-looking guy I hadn't seen in more than a year. I'd had a big crush on him. He was charming with the cutest side dimple. I started to say hello before interrupting myself.

Grace! Remember what you saw in the mirror today? Do yourself a favor and hide. And whatever you do, do NOT let him see you like this.

So I hid. And the really good-looking guy bought his coffee and left.

I returned to my journal, asking God to teach me something new. I had been at a standstill with Him lately. I wasn't happy. I was confused, actually. God confused me. I was tired of being single. And insecurity had crept into my life once again, causing me to feel inadequate.

What was my purpose? Why was I here? Why did I have 535 pimples on my face? Why didn't I feel like I fit in?

I was tired of striving to please the world, yet at the same time addicted to trying. I couldn't help but think, *Am I ever going to be enough?*

That's when I heard another gal talking in a sort-of-whisper voice. When I looked toward the voice, I saw a beautiful girl wearing a blue sweater. She had a friend with her, and they were trying not to be heard.

Challenge accepted. My curiosity tends to get the best of me, and if they were talking in hushed tones, the conversation had to be worth hearing, right?

Blue Sweater Girl was talking about her heart being broken.

"I guess I just wasn't enough for him," I heard her say. She appeared to be crying. "I stalked his new girl, and she is *way* hotter than me."

I got so mad at her I nearly interrupted, "Girl, have you read the Bible? You *are* enough!"

But I sensed Jesus stopping me and humbling me: *Grace, you had the same thoughts as her about five minutes ago.*

Ouch.

How quickly I had forgotten about not talking to a guy I'd been friends with, and only because I didn't think I was pretty enough in that moment to say hello.

I had allowed a lie to control my actions. I'd allowed a lie to make me insecure. And even though I thought I knew the truth, I was just as lost as Blue Sweater Girl as she cried over the guy who left her for some other chick, leaving only a broken heart behind.

We forget how common it is, as young ladies, to believe these lies every day. We forget how difficult it is to be a girl.

We grow up thinking we are princesses until around age thirteen, when we learn the painful lesson that we aren't the prettiest girl in the world. That we're not the smartest person in our grade. And then there's the discovery that really hurts: not everyone wants to be our friend.

High school didn't turn out to be *High School Musical.* We graduate and move on to college and young adulthood, only to find that our twenties are not necessarily the best years of our lives, and that even someone as great as Elle Woods at one point dates a not-so-great guy like Warner.

Soon enough, we're hiding underneath a hat, avoiding the world because we don't feel "enough." Like Blue Sweater Girl, we find ourselves brokenhearted because we believe we aren't "enough" for this world.

We wonder, and we struggle. We wrestle with insecurity and wind up asking ourselves, "Am I enough?"

On days like that, we need to get out from under our cap, forget about what we looked like in the mirror, look up, and say "hello" to God. God did not call you to hide from life when you have a bad hair day. God did not create you to hide on days you don't feel adequate. God called you to a life of love and service, to live in a way that points to Him.

On those "I can't do today" days when I want to hide from all social interaction, I remember my life is meant to be a reflection of Him. What if Esther had thought she had too many pimples to approach the king and save the lives of His chosen people? What if Mary had cared too much about what people thought about her being unmarried and having a child? What if you spend an hour worrying about your appearance and miss an opportunity to shine for Him?

Obviously, this is deeper than talking to a cute crush. This is about whether we are using every second to bring Him praise or if we are too busy hiding because we don't feel "enough."

Matthew 5:14–16 says:

You are the light of the world. A town built on a hill cannot be hidden. Neither do people light a lamp and put it under a bowl. Instead they put it on its stand, and it gives light to everyone in the house. In the same way, let your light shine before others, that they may see your good deeds and glorify your Father in heaven.

Be bold and confident. Walk with the truth that even though you consider today a bad hair day, God can use you. He uses women with acne and women with complicated pasts. Your light should not be hidden. You should not be too timid to live your life because of insecurities. So forget about your insecurity and shine your light for your Creator. God is trying to use you, so stop hiding.

Real Talk

- Do you ever shy away from doing something you want to or you think is right because you do not feel "enough"?
- Whose approval do you find yourself most often seeking?
- What does it mean to be a friend of the world, and where does that lead?
- Pray and ask God to reveal to you areas in which you are hung up on not being "enough." Ask God to speak to those areas.

Chapter 10

15 Things I'd Rather Be Than Hot

*I*was washing my hands in a restaurant bathroom when two females my age came strolling in. They took their places in front of the mirror, not turning to face each other as they talked. One started pulling on her arms to show her friend her arm fat. The second did the same with her own arms.

"Life would be so much easier if I was as hot as a model," one said.

For about ten seconds, I silently agreed.

If I looked like a Victoria's Secret model, I thought, *I bet that baseball player in English class would talk to me for more than the ten seconds it takes him to ask to borrow a pen. Every single day. I'm running out of pens—and opportunities for him to flirt with me.*

My next thought showed just how much I had been influenced by the significance the world places on looks.

If only I was hotter, life would be twenty times better.

Wrong! At about the eleventh second of those thoughts, I realized the error in my thinking. Being hot is the wrong objective. So, I made a list of the fifteen things I would rather be than hot.

1. Eager

Each morning when I hear my annoying alarm, I wake up and pray that I can be more eager. Whether walking to an 8 a.m. class or driving to work, I want to be eager for the adventures and the beautiful possibilities that can occur at any given moment. My prayer is that I can look to God and thank him for another day of new mercies and a chance to love like never before. I pray that I am eager to be who God created me to be—eager to love and eager to serve. That is my hope each morning.

2. Cultured

I want to see the world the Lord created more than I want to be accepted by the world. I want to talk to people from all over the globe and hear their stories. This suburban girl wants to experience life in other people's shoes, get to know different cultures, and learn something new from everyone I meet.

One of the greatest gifts God grants us is our ability to have relationships. I strive for relationships with people who don't look like me. It doesn't require a long cruise to experience the world; a friendly greeting to spark conversations with people we haven't met can help us achieve that right around the corner.

3. A living sacrifice

I want my body to be used as a vessel for God's glory, not turning on guys. I want to dedicate my body to being a spiritual act of worship, with every breath of energy the Lord gives me praising

His name. Our bodies have never been our own; God created and designed them, and they are to be used for His purpose. May we glorify the One who gave His body on a cross so that we can experience salvation.

4. A fighter

I have no desire to fight a gal who annoys me, or even one who is mean to me. But I believe it's beautiful to see a woman who fights her insecurities and the lies the enemy tells her daily. A truly beautiful woman fights off those lies and life's troubles by filling her soul with Scripture. "Here on earth you will have many trials and sorrows" (John 16:33, NLT). Those are Jesus' words, not mine. We're going to hurt. We're going to suffer heartbreak. There will be tears. However, we're not defined by our own strength during those trials; we are defined by whether we choose to tap into the strength that our Savior has made available to fight those battles.

5. A teacher

I want to teach others through my actions and words. I want to acquire wisdom more than a good body. I want anyone who encounters me to learn about love, humor, and how fun it is to live with the Savior in my heart. I want everyone who knows me to feel better for having known me.

6. A learner

Teaching requires learning. I want each sunrise to bring a new chance for me to grow in knowledge and craft. Each night when I go to bed, I want to be able to say that I advanced my knowledge to the fullest potential that day. I want to learn from others who have walked the path ahead of me. Most important, I want to go to class with the Lord each day, eagerly sitting up front, ready to hear the truth He pours into His students by simply standing before us. I want to learn from the King of kings.

I also would like to learn to moonwalk like Michael Jackson before I die. That is way cooler than being hot.

7. Confident

Being confident is not a bad thing—there is a difference between confident and cocky. A woman needs to be confident enough to love herself first before anyone else loves her. Awareness of worth leads to becoming a happier person who can conquer any challenges. We cannot truly love our Creator without loving the image of Him we see in the mirror.

8. Joyful

Joy is my favorite part of the fruit of the Spirit. Nothing is quite as beautiful as waking up every morning, regardless of whatever trials may be coming in the day ahead, with the knowledge that the Lord has blessed me with a new day and a purpose greater than looking great. Joy is contagious, and the ability to pass it along to those around us is an amazing opportunity.

9. A friend

I want to be loyal to those God has placed alongside me. I want to do life with many people, investing time and energy into meaningful conversations. Sometimes the best feeling in the world comes from eating Chinese takeout with girlfriends and talking about exes and new cute dresses while watching *Mean Girls* for the 32,424th time. I hope to enjoy many moments of friendship like that in my life.

10. A hiker

My dad counts his pennies and finds ways around spending money on things he considers "useless." I have many memories of my dad sprinting through the streets on family vacations, refusing to pay for a cab, while my mom and I huffed and puffed as we tried to keep up. Personally, I prefer calling Uber over taking a long walk.

So I don't want to hike the highest mountains. Instead, I want to go through each of my trials with the agility to overcome even my most difficult battles. I want to hike all the way to the peak, where I can breathe the freshest air, gazing out over the valleys of my life. I want to be able to say with all certainty that I ran the race set before me. That I made it through all the lows. That I never gave up. And then from that peak, I will see what God had planned for me, and that He was with me all along the way. "The Sovereign LORD is my strength; he makes my feet like the feet of a deer, he enables me to tread on the heights" (Habakkuk 3:19).

11. Servant-hearted

I want to use my hands and feet for a purpose greater than meeting my needs. To me, acting in compassion is one of the most beautiful things we can do because it demonstrates love for others and for God. I would much rather be known for giving to others than for maintaining an attractive appearance.

12. Dependent

Why would I tell young women they need to be dependent? I get it—this is the modern world, and the message now is that women do not need to depend on men.

I am an independent person. As soon as I could drive, I got

a job as a waitress in a sushi restaurant so I could have my own money to spend. When it came to choosing a college, I decided to attend one six hundred miles from home.

I don't want to depend on a man or any other person. But I do want to be completely dependent upon God. I want to remember that the presence of God is a necessity, not a luxury. I want my eyes to open each morning looking toward Him. I want to go to God for every little moment in my life.

God doesn't call us to say, "Hey, man, I've got this on my own." We don't. In fact, that's impossible. God wants us to understand and act on our deep need for Him every day.

13. Funny

When I'm eighty, I won't look the same as I do now. I'll have more wrinkles and sags and droops. But I will always have my sense of humor. I would rather be known for being funny and having a contagious laugh than for looking hot. Even if I am the only one who thinks I am funny, I don't care. Okay, maybe it would be nice to have other people think I'm funny, but if worse comes to worst, at least they may think it is funny that I think I am funny. (Close enough?)

14. Someone who leaves a legacy

News flash: we will all die. When I die, I want this world to be a better place because my life reflected God every day to those around me. I care more about building a legacy of love than about being known as an attractive girl or as eye-candy for guys. I hope people will remember me not for my looks, but because I loved and was kind to others.

15. A dancer

Perhaps you post cool videos of yourself dancing on Instagram. Or perhaps you're like me and did that growing up, but now the thought of dancing makes you want to barf because you have noodle arms. If you're more like me, take heart, because the dancing I'm talking about requires no minimum skill level.

I'm talking about dancing with the great I Am. When we follow His lead, He will take our hands and lead us into a beautiful journey where we can simply glide where He wants us to go. That kind of dance is so beautiful that others can't help but stop and stare and want to dance like that as well.

The next time I feel like fussing to the mirror about how I look, I hope the Holy Spirit interrupts and causes me to ask myself, "How can I better fulfill God's purpose for me?"

Then with that attitude, perhaps I'll ask Jesus to dance with me. I think I know His answer.

Real Talk

- Which of those fifteen characteristics spoke to you most?
- Do you find yourself focusing on your looks instead of focusing on becoming a better disciple?
- When you die, what do you hope to have accomplished that will impact someone else's eternity?
- Pray and ask God to help you create a list of characteristics that are important to Him.

Chapter 11

Remember the Most
Important Part

*I*served as an intern at my home church during my senior year of high school. One time, the church needed somewhere around one hundred letters mailed to people who donated to a mission trip. My friend Logan and I teamed up for the assignment. Logan was in charge of placing stamps and address labels on the envelopes. My job was to stuff and lick the envelopes.

We cranked up the country music in our workroom and set up our assembly line. We quickly found our groove and couldn't believe how rapidly we were getting the job done. We might have been the best duo ever in the history of envelope stuffing!

My tongue was starting to dry out from all the envelope licking, but the stack of envelopes was down to about twenty, so I knew my tongue would soon have its needed—and well-earned—relief.

That's when I felt Logan staring at me from the side. I looked at him and smiled, rather pleased with our progress.

"Whatcha looking at?" I asked.

"Grace," he said, then paused. "Have you been stuffing the envelopes?"

Big oops!

After the first letter, I forgot an important part of the process: actually stuffing the letters inside the envelopes. Thus, approximately seventy-nine licked and sealed envelopes were missing letters. The people who had helped make the mission trip possible were on the verge of receiving empty envelopes as our church's expression of gratitude.

I had become so determined to work quickly, on getting through the project, that I forgot the most important point of the project. I had been so focused on the destination that I had allowed myself to get sidetracked during the journey.

Logan and I laughed. I can't remember who laughed first, but I sure was glad Logan found humor in the situation. In good spirits, both of us set to work fixing *my* mistake.

The lesson learned that day was to slow down and to enjoy this journey called life. To stop rushing and to make sure to savor the everyday moments that too often pass by unnoticed. Instead of looking all the way to the end of the project, I need to focus on how God wants to use me in this very second.

God has our futures planned. We need to stop worrying about our plans not going the way we imagine. Seriously, do we not trust the Author of this life to write our stories?

You and I are called to be where we are right now for a reason. Maybe you've heard the saying, "You are called to bloom where you are planted." This means rooting ourselves in the place we are right now, in the very second we are living. Not getting too far ahead of ourselves, but focusing on the present—the here and now.

The stage of life you are in right now is crucial to the development of the final product. Focus on exalting God and drawing close to the Son. If a flower is not seeded properly, no root can sprout. If the root is not sprouted correctly, no stem can grow. If the stem does not grow properly, no flower can bloom.

Stop rushing life. Loosen the grip on your five-year plan and latch on to the One who custom-designed a plan for you. If you rush through every day, you miss out on savoring where God currently has you. If you get so preoccupied with the end of the road and forget to pray along the way, you are forgetting the most important part of the process. Focus every drop of energy into communicating with your Creator.

Life may not be going the way you want. Perhaps you don't have the friendships, relationships, jobs, or circumstances you'd planned for. Perhaps you want to rush through this stage of your life to get to what you hope will be better days. Instead, hold on. Wait to see what God is teaching you.

And most of all, bloom where you are planted. God wants to use you right where you are.

Real Talk

- Do you find yourself rushing too much through life?
- What are three things you think you have missed out on in your past by rushing?
- What does "blooming where you're planted" look like for the stage of life you're in?
- How can you more fully enjoy the everyday moments with your Creator?
- Pray and thank God for all the everyday moments he places along your path.

LIE #5

Numbers are the judge of beauty.

Chapter 12

The Weight of the World

My legs felt like they were about to fall off. I was sixteen and had just attended spin class and BODYPUMP, then spent thirty minutes on the elliptical at a level way higher than my legs were ready for. I had brushed off lunch to go to a class with my broadcast friends, and I ate only a LUNA Bar. I was fine. Totally fine. That's what I told myself.

But as I stepped off the elliptical, my legs felt separated from my body. My thighs were shaking as I got into my car and went home. I ate dinner that night, but not too long after I was at the toilet. I made myself throw up my food. I usually only focused on watching what I ate and worked out an unhealthy amount. But this time, I felt as if I needed to get everything out of my system. I threw up and kept trying to throw up more. After all my dinner had left my stomach, I began to dry heave and cry. I knew I had gone too far.

I was not fine.

I thought back to a conversation with a teacher that day at school.

I'd worn a skin-tight jacket that caused everyone in my class to notice my suddenly thin frame. I received a shower of compliments about my weight loss.

Except from one teacher. She seemed to know something was up and called me out of class to talk.

"Grace, are you being healthy?" she asked. "All you talk about is working out and you have lost a lot of weight. Teachers don't really see you eating at lunch and, honestly, I'm worried. Are you okay? You know you are beautiful and don't have to do this."

I told the teacher I was fine, just . . . as I'd told myself many times. But that night as I hit rock bottom in my bathroom, I admitted I wasn't fine. This teacher was right. I needed to change.

Obsession with my weight has been front and center when I've wrestled the most with my insecurity. I've allowed the numbers on my scale to dictate my emotions, and I've read seemingly every article on weight loss I could find.

My obsession with my weight came down to two desires:

1. To look good in a swimsuit.
2. For guys to think I was attractive.

During one two-month period during high school, I dropped from 132 pounds and a size 4 to 104 pounds and a size 0.

My obsessions drove me to work out at least two-and-a-half hours every day at the gym. I wouldn't leave until I had burned a minimum of 800 calories. I made myself look busy so I could skip lunch. I occasionally treated a 100-calorie granola bar as a meal. I intensely focused on projects and activities so I wouldn't hear my stomach growling. I'd stop eating halfway through dinner and mumble about hating the food, even though that wasn't true.

My goal was to lose as much weight as I could as quickly as I could, and I did. By the world's definition, I looked "good." I was skinny enough.

That one conversation with my teacher stuck with me. It made me realize that I had gone too far with dieting. I broke down in the gym bathroom that night, crying over the error of my ways. I had lost twenty-eight pounds and dropped four sizes. Friends were complimenting me, yet it still wasn't enough to boost my opinion of myself.

I weigh 145 pounds as I write this, and I have the confidence to post that number in a book for all to see. That number would have haunted me in high school. I still occasionally struggle with my perception of my weight when I look in the mirror, but it's much better than it used to be. God has helped me learn to accept my body and enjoy a Chick-fil-A chocolate milkshake every now and then. I work out when I have time, but not like my life depends on it. I eat a normal and healthy calorie intake, and carbs no longer send me into panic. (In fact, I love carbs. Pizza is life!)

My obsession with my weight was not healthy physically or emotionally. I know many of you have experienced the same problem. I've watched friends skip meals to shed a few pounds before a formal. I've seen friends sip on Jamba Juice as if that small 300-calorie smoothie with little to no protein powder contained enough fuel to get them through the day. I've had friends try every new detox and weird wrap, and overwork in the gym for the sole purpose of looking good in a bikini.

Based on my experience, I think the problem comes down to two things. One is neglecting the truth that embracing God's love is more important than becoming a size 0. The second is that we as women tend to find more worth in what the scale tells us than what Scripture tells us.

Okay, so maybe a guy dumped you or said you weren't good enough for him. But God's Word says you are altogether beautiful. The scale tells you that you have more pounds to shed. But Scripture says to stop focusing on the world. The world says you can become more beautiful. But God says He created you in His image—and that is enough.

If you have a friend who you believe is too obsessed with her weight, have the courage to let your friend know you care about her health more than how she looks. Don't stop yourself because you think it isn't your business. Friends speak the truth in love. You might even be saving your friend's life.

I regret not speaking out sooner. Until my teacher steered me back onto the right path, no one knew how insecure I was. I had my internship at the church, I led a Bible study and morning devotion at a café, I was class president, I was on the homecoming and prom courts, and I was voted Miss Fontainebleau High School. Name an award at school, and I was least in the running to win it. I looked completely happy on the outside. But inside I was a teenage girl still struggling with insecurities caused by comments from some mean middle school bullies.

I couldn't control the face they made fun of, but I could control my weight. Skinnier, I believed, would equal prettier. I posted bikini photos on Instagram that received a ton of likes. Compliments became an addiction. "How did you get so toned and skinny?" "You are so skinny. Can you tell me how to get as skinny as you?"

In spite of all that, I didn't like my body. By extension, I didn't like myself. I'd wanted to be skinny enough for people to notice me, yet when I reached that point, it wasn't enough. If someone said I looked great, I felt like I needed to look perfect. Let me tell you, chasing perfection will only leave you out of breath and disappointed. Perfect is unobtainable.

At your funeral, the preacher isn't going to say through tears, "Wow! Ashley had the best bod ever!" Your favorite aunt won't tell her church congregation that you had "one of the hottest bodies she has ever seen." Besides, would you really want that to be how people remember you? Wouldn't it be better for the preacher of your funeral to talk about how much you loved Jesus and those around you? Or for your aunt to tell her church about the joy you carried daily, and your ability to make others smile?

I know I don't want my tombstone to read, "Here lies Grace, who once had a six-pack."

If this chapter touched home for you, I hope you'll accept this challenge: stop focusing on your physical looks more than your internal look. To help do that, feed yourself the fruit of the Spirit. Fill up on Scripture.

Your worth is not based on the numbers on the scale. That's the truth—I know it's difficult to believe, but you must. Instead of doing that juice cleanse to flush out fat before your beach trip, flush out your insecurity, your desire to gossip, and your belief that you aren't enough.

Diet that way.

Also, try this workout plan.

Don't focus on having arms that are perfectly toned, but on having arms that serve God and others. Instead of a six-pack for that way-too-small bikini, work on developing a stomach filled with healthy food and belly laughs. Rather than aiming for the legs of a Victoria's Secret model, decide to have legs that dance with the Lord and follow where He leads.

Yes, go ahead and eat fresh fruit, go for a long run, and do your squats. But never, ever let the scale determine your sense of worth. That number on your scale is just that—a number—but your relationship with Christ is your destiny:

> Your beauty should not come from outward adornment, such as elaborate hairstyles and the wearing of gold jewelry or fine clothes. Rather, it should be that of your inner self, the unfading beauty of a gentle and quiet spirit, which is of great worth in God's sight. (1 Peter 3:3–4)

Real Talk

- What is your biggest insecurity regarding your body?
- What do you think God would say about that insecurity?
- Do you have a friend who you think is letting the scale determine her self-worth? What is keeping you from telling her you care about her and are concerned about her health? What could happen if you don't talk to her about this?
- Write a prayer thanking God for handcrafting you in His image. Ask Him to remind you to focus on your inner self before you focus on your body.

Chapter 13

Meeting Jessica

My freshman year of college, I showed my hairdresser the selfie of a gal I'll call Jessica.

"Can I get my hair done like this?" I asked.

Jessica had the perfect life, body, and hair—and a thigh gap. The guys who took her out on dates were good looking themselves. And she had a cute puppy.

All that *and* a cute puppy?

I'd never met Jessica; I'd only followed her on Instagram. But I wanted to wake up the next morning as Jessica. I wanted her life instead of mine.

My hairdresser gave me the highlights and lowlights to match Jessica's hair color. To my disappointment, when my hairdresser removed the smock, I still was me. As if a couple of additional strawberry blonde streaks were all that separated me from Jessica.

Jessicas are all over social media. We stalk them not because we want to be friends with them, but because we want to *be* them.

I used to spend too many days comparing myself to different

Jessicas. They had abs, toned arms, and the perfect life. Then I obsessed over who I was on social media. I'd wonder whether my ex-boyfriend would see my selfies, think I was hot, and miss me. I'd wonder if other girls thought I was cool. Did they want to be me? I'd constantly change or fine-tune my profile pic, hoping Tim Tebow would find me and scroll to learn more. I wanted my life to look as cool on social media as Jessica from Instagram. But no matter how many times I highlighted my hair Jessica's color, I couldn't be her.

Then, one day, I met Jessica. It turned out we attended the same university, and she sat down next to me in a class. We even became friends. We laughed at celebrity gossip, discussed our love for Elle Woods, and studied together in the library. One day I was complaining about my makeup, my skin, and my body, so I said something like, "I need to shed ten pounds and figure out how to actually contour."

"Ugh. Me too," Jessica said. "I feel like a whale."

Whoa! Jessica thought she needed to lose weight? Could she, of all people, possibly have felt insecure? My friend I wanted to be like struggled with feeling not "enough"? But she was living the perfect life. Her Instagram feed made it look like she had it all. I assumed she was confident. But, I was learning, Jessica was just like me. She was struggling with insecurities and the feeling of not being enough.

I wish I could say I informed Jessica her worth comes from Christ. But at that time, I hadn't discovered that about myself yet. I was blind to the truth because I was still comparing my looks to women like Jessica.

Comparison is the thief of joy because it tends to highlight others' best moments while reminding you of your worst. It's also a difficult habit to break. You compare yourself to someone like Jessica on social media one day and the next thing you know, you're on some fashion blogger's account who has an even better body—and an even better life. You dig a little deeper into her posts and find out she also has a boyfriend and a puppy. Then you go to the gym and compare your body to the fit girl on the next elliptical. And she's on level 17 with an incline while you're huffing and puffing on 5.

Let's be real. The woman you stalk on Instagram has days when she doesn't feel attractive. She's struggling to find her true worth. Her relationship you wish you had isn't all blueberry-picking dates and expensive dinners with wine. Sometimes she and her boyfriend have late-night arguments and take an eight o'clock trip to Chick-fil-A because dinner burned again.

Deep down, the girl in the top sorority craves friends who actually care for her. She barely acknowledges you and your friends, but when you walk past she envies the friendship you share.

And as I learned, even Jessicas deal with problems. If we sit down and talk—*really* talk—with those whom we assume have it all together, we'll see that they actually are the same as us in many ways. They've been broken, they still see themselves in their awkward middle school years, and they get pimples even though they're twenty-five. Who knows? If you tell them about your insecurities, you might hear them say, "Me too."

In fact, you would probably have a difficult time trying to find another woman who hasn't felt inadequate. Yet, social media has become a mask where we talk only about what shapes an image we want to cast—we got the job, we aced the test, we bought a new car. But not until we whitened our teeth and edited our arms on four different apps before posting the picture.

Our lives weren't meant to be perfect, nor were they intended to be filtered. We are broken and flawed. All of us. There will always be another girl who has something that's better. Yet we keep living in competition.

Why do we live like life is a contest? If we want to compete so badly, here's a competition worth entering: "Everyone who competes in the games goes into strict training. They do it to get a crown that will not last, but we do it to get a crown that will last forever" (1 Corinthians 9:25).

There's two races in this world you can run:

1. You can chase the world.
2. You can chase Jesus.

You can't run both races. They are two conflicting events going on at the same time. You have to decide which race you will run. Are you going to spend your life striving to be like every girl you stalk on social media? Or are you going to chase your Savior who holds the ultimate prize—eternity—by His side?

If you spend your life chasing the Jessicas of the world, you will lose the race. You were never meant to be Jessica. You were never meant to be compared to your ex's new girlfriend.

But if you chase Jesus, you will realize that although you are not enough for the world, you are enough for your Savior. If you chase Jesus, you will realize that your worth comes from whose you are and not who you are.

So let's strive to seek after Jesus. Run the race toward eternity. Stop playing the comparison game. Start chasing Jesus. Compete for something that actually carries meaning.

Real Talk

- How often do you compare yourself to others on social media?
- What prize should you be competing for?
- How can you use social media to connect instead of compare?
- Pray for women you often find yourself competing with in your mind. You might be the only person praying for them.

Chapter 14

The Ultimate Diet

I was nineteen and getting ready for my formal. I thought I had finally found a dress for the event—until I saw the photo of me wearing it. Then I found something worse than the dress when I zoomed in on one of my arms—it looked as wide as my hips.

Tears started falling.

I can't look like this. I'm so . . . fat. Am I really supposed to show up to my formal looking like this?

Thus began my Google search for a diet that would solve all my problems. Thanks to this soon-to-be-found diet, the scale would reveal my true worth. I just knew the diet I was searching for would make me pretty enough by spring break. Then, guys would gawk at me at the beach. The ones who decided I wasn't good enough for them would regret having passed me by.

In the end, however, my search for the ultimate diet turned out to be rather strange. There was the "army diet," the "no carbs/protein diet," and—major eye roll coming—the "only avocado diet." I decided to say no to those diets. Based on my past struggles with dieting and an eating disorder, I knew they were not the answer. I searched for a solution that would actually make me feel better, and I finally found it. The best diet I can recommend calls for the removal of these things in your life:

1. The guy who makes you feel worthless

It's time to let go of all the pain he brings into your life. Whatever he told you—they're lies. Delete his number, delete his Snapchat. Now. No longer allow yourself to be played by a guy who doesn't realize how beautiful you are.

If you continue looking back into your past, you might never notice the blessings in front of you. Your ex is your ex for a reason. If you had an "almost" relationship, it wasn't a real relationship for a reason.

You deserve a guy who won't make you feel insecure.

2. Your competitiveness with other girls

Life is not a contest based on who can get more guys or who is prettier. Be happy for those around you when good things happen to them. Don't envy them or try to outdo them for the sake of competition. Guess what? You'll always find someone skinner and prettier than you. That's life. All you can do is be the best you possible.

Ladies, we know how hard it is to be a woman in this world. So why do we allow ourselves to put more pain on ourselves and other women? Focus on the race God has called you to—the one that leads you closer to Jesus. The one we just talked about. And stop trying to race against those who are supposed to be your teammates.

3. Your desire for a guy in your life

As cheesy as it sounds, the best relationships often come when we aren't expecting them. If you are single and don't want to be, trust God's timing. He will write your beautiful love story. Actually, He's already written it. He's just allowing your story to unfold so you can appreciate it more.

Stop checking your phone every minute to see if the hot guy you're crushing on liked your latest Instagram photo. Attract guys with your personality—not your body—and then seal the deal with the kind of internal beauty that's irresistible because it's genuine. Who wants to say at your wedding, "Well, uh, he liked the photo of me in a bikini and then slid in my DMs"? Come on—you know you're worth more than that!

4. Thinking that a good body will fix everything

Impressive abs and a good body don't solve the problems of insecurity. You know that part of my story. Don't expect to finally be happy because your stomach is tighter. Stop searching for the world to satisfy you when you were not created for the world. The only thing that can satisfy you is the One who breathed life into you.

5. The friend who is not really a friend

Your friendships affect your thoughts, so be on guard against any relationship that only brings you down. A true friend doesn't belittle you or make you feel insecure. Someone who gossips to you might cause you to gossip as well. Someone who routinely insults others to you will probably insult you to others.

I'm not saying to completely cut the cord with such a "friend." Try having an honest conversation first in which you say you're no longer comfortable or interested in conversations that involve gossip. If she doesn't change, that doesn't mean you have to be mean along with her. Pray for her.

Be intentional to surround yourself with people who point you to Christ, not cause you to stray. Joy is contagious, but so is sin. Love yourself enough to spend time with friends who push you to walk with Jesus, strive to be a better person each day, and live a life that builds people up instead of tears them down.

Real Talk

- What else do you need to eliminate from your "diet"?
- What causes you to hang on to a guy who makes you feel insecure?
- What is wrong with placing too much emphasis on how your body looks?
- If a close friend whom you trusted told you that she has observed one of your relationships bringing you down, how would you receive that?
- Pray to be satisfied with how God made you.

LIE #6

God just wants to be your friend.

Chapter 15

Stop Friend-Zoning God

The friend zone.

It is so frustrating when you are interested in a guy and he friend-zones you. For some reason, I go way back into my childhood when I think about friend-zoning, even though back then we had yet to establish the name for that dreaded place.

Lizzie McGuire was my favorite TV show growing up. Lizzie (Hilary Duff) was oblivious to the fact that Gordo (Adam Lamberg) liked her. Gordo was always there for Lizzie, and I mean always. They had been friends since they were babies. But for most of the series, Lizzie considered Gordo "just a friend" and didn't seem to notice how Gordo felt about her.

That's friend-zoning. It's something we do in romantic relationships, but it's also something we do to God.

God and Gordo

What does it look like for us to friend-zone God?

Well, we know God, don't we? But do we actually *know* Him? Do we communicate with Him daily? Do we spend enough time studying His Word so that we know His personality, His characteristics? Or do we just talk to Him when we need Him or spend just enough time reading the Bible to say we do when asked?

Yes, God is always there when we need Him, just like Gordo was always there for Lizzie. But when we don't "need" God, are we content to keep the relationship at a lower level than He desires? Do we not talk to Him and not study Scripture to the point that we become oblivious to how much more He wants from our relationship? If something of the world that's really attractive comes along, do we worship it more than God? I'd be lying if I said I've never left God hanging for a cute guy with good hair.

Let's explore one more area of questions. Would you give your life for God? I think most believers would say that we would if confronted with a situation where someone pointed a gun to our head and demanded that we deny God or lose our life. Part of the reason most of us would say yes is because it's an extreme hypothetical situation that none of us is likely to face. Plus, when considering that question, it seems noble to die because we wouldn't deny God.

But how often do we deny Him in ways that aren't immediately life-threatening? It could happen when a coworker uses His name in vain, and we say nothing. It could happen when a guy wants to take a relationship to a physical level that goes against God's Word. It could be at a party when a friend asks if we want to try something that will make us feel really good.

Those are the times when it's easiest to keep God in the friend zone. Those are the times when we don't want the type of relationship that is based on a love that provokes change. Friend-zoning God is keeping control of our lives so that we can do whatever we want and still say that we know Him. It's a less-risky relationship for us.

Only the Lonely

When I battled against loneliness, I would ask God why I didn't have friends who cared about me. I didn't feel like I fit in with any group or clique, and I didn't understand why. I needed friends to be happy. Now I realize that I was searching for people who could make me happy when only God could give me the joy I was missing. God wired us to live in community, and He desires for us to find loving Christian friends. However, we can still encounter seasons of loneliness when we think that finding joy is dependent upon our popularity.

Jesus was lonely at times. He didn't emerge from His loneliness by trying to become popular. In fact, during times of loneliness, He often did things that were the opposite of what might have made Him popular. Instead, He would go off by Himself to pray, and that would give Him strength. Although lonely, Jesus never strayed from His mission. He never friend-zoned His heavenly Father, and we should follow that example.

When we combat loneliness by doing what this world says, we are friend-zoning the only One who can satisfy us. That only compounds whatever problems we are facing.

The world tries to portray God in ways that would keep us from believing He wants to be much more than our friend. Some of those false portraits paint God as an authoritative ruler, or someone who's so far removed from us that He doesn't understand how we feel. Referring to God as "The Man Upstairs" is wrong for various reasons. For starters, God doesn't want to live a floor above us; He wants to take up full-time residence in our hearts.

We need to commit to no longer friend-zoning God. We need to stop ignoring His requests to pursue Him to the degree He pursues us. We need to stop chasing the ways of the world and leave God "over there," even as He cares for us while we live in ways He wants to help us change.

God created us with free will. He has given us the freedom to eye what the world offers. If you're looking in that direction, I pray that you will turn your eyes toward Him and recognize that He is the only one who can satisfy your desire to feel pursued. He's not just pursuing you; He's pursuing you with a perfect, unconditional love.

Despite your imperfections, He loves you, desires you, and is calling out for you to remove Him from the friend zone. He has the answers to the questions you're asking. He can satisfy what you are pursing.

But you need to stop liking Him and start loving Him.

Real Talk

- In what ways have you friend-zoned God?
- How do you think God feels about being friend-zoned by His creation?
- How can you pursue God more in your everyday life?
- Write a prayer to God asking to learn more about Him, and for a stronger and deeper relationship than you've ever had with Him.

Chapter 16

Mean What You Say

I had a friend who repeatedly talked negatively about me behind my back. She would apologize, we'd have a good moment together, and then she would go right back to running me down to others.

But one time, she apologized differently than before. I approached her after learning that she had told a guy I was a prude and made fun of me for my decision not to have sex before marriage. I told her she should have respected my decision instead of mocking me for it.

"I'm sorry, Grace," she said. I'd heard that a few times before. Except she added, "I really am this time." Then she flipped her hair and returned to working on her laptop. Whatever was on that screen seemed more important to her than my feelings.

Even though we'd been through this song and dance previously, I wanted to believe her.

"But do you promise to not do this again?" I asked. "Do you

promise to not talk about me and to be a friend who cares for me from now on?"

I desperately wanted her to say yes. She looked me directly in the eyes and, for the first time, spoke truthfully with me.

"Honestly, Grace, I am sorry when I talk about you. But everyone talks about everyone, and I can't promise that I won't talk about you in a mean way ever again. This is what girls do."

My translation: "Yep. I feel bad, but I'll probably do this again." *What?!? Is that how "I'm sorry" works now?*

At this point in the story, she probably sounds like the villain to you. It felt that way to me too. But as is so often the case with those types of moments, the Holy Spirit convicted me for my own similar attitude.

As ridiculous as the girl's answer was, I realized that many times my actions were no different than her words. I would feel the guilt and say I'm sorry, but I'd move on without correcting my behavior.

Through my dog poop–scraping community service, I learned about how undeserving we are and how beautiful God's covenant love can be if we choose to embrace it. But that can lead to another problem I have struggled with: taking advantage of God's grace.

Drinking Problems

Alcohol has been a problem like that for me. Even though I knew the Holy Spirit convicted me to stop drinking, I tried to rationalize myself into a place where alcohol was okay for me. I looked for excuses that would allow me to keep drinking.

I was selfish. I wanted things to go the way I wanted.

I would use the old reliable "but Jesus drank wine" line and act like that covered taking ten vodka shots and doing a keg stand. (Yeah, Jesus didn't do *that*.)

I especially struggled with alcohol during my freshman year of college. I thought downing shots would make me cool. It made talking to guys easier.

I would drown myself with shots on Saturday and go to church on Sunday. I would tell God that I was sorry and suffer through the guilt. Then on Thursday, I'd start feeling insecure again as the weekend approached and think a shot or two or five could make me feel better. Then I'd wake up wondering what happened the night before.

Even though I would black out, I had decided I would never do anything that was "bad." As if that makes sense. Fortunately, I never had the experience of waking up and finding out that a guy had taken advantage of my drunkenness.

Sometimes the guilt would cause me to give up alcohol for a month, or maybe even a whole semester. But I'd eventually hop right back in that cycle. All the while, I was telling God I was sorry and doing nothing about it.

One night, I drove my own car to where my friends were because I knew I shouldn't be drinking anymore and I wanted my own ride home if I decided to leave. I didn't like who I had become as a drinker, and I recognized that God had better plans for me and my body than to be a zombie controlled by alcohol. There was more to life than hangovers and heartbreak.

"Grace Valentine!" someone yelled. "Take a drink right now!"

I laughed. "I'm driving tonight, or I would."

Well, it wasn't long after that when I was raising my own shot glass alongside my friends' glasses. The last thing I remember thinking that night was: *God will forgive me. It's okay.*

Once again I was fortunate, because someone picked me up and drove me home. I passed out on my couch. The next morning, I woke up with the worst hangover. I went to work and had to throw up in the bathroom. I lay on the cold tile floor next to the toilet and puked my guts out. A guy I'd had a crush on walked into the bathroom right in the middle of me vomiting. That scratched his name off the "possibles" list. (God obviously has a sense of humor.)

In my hungover state, my mind went back to the last thought I remembered from the night before: *God will forgive me. It's okay.*

It was as if the serpent from the Garden of Eden had slithered into my mind and convinced me to drink that first shot. And then the next. And then the next. And then the tenth.

It's just a drink, I could imagine him telling me. *God won't care. He can forgive you.*

Forbidden Fruit

When Adam and Eve ate from the tree of the knowledge of good and evil in the Garden of Eden, they did so even though God had specifically instructed them not to.

My forbidden fruit of choice was alcohol. I knew God had called me to stop drinking, but I took advantage of His grace in order to numb my social anxiety.

We all have forbidden fruit. It might be weed, sex, or the guy you know is no good for you. Your sin of choice could be gossip, immodest fashion choices, or stealing. It could be pride in thinking

114

that you are better than the girl whose sin of choice seems worse than yours.

For those who need to admit this, I'll hope you'll be like me and confess that you are guilty of taking advantage of God's grace.

Realizing a decision is wrong is not the same as asking for forgiveness. You can realize you made a bad choice without being sorry and apologizing for it.

Being sorry means that if you could go back and change your decision, you would—that you desire not to make the same mistake next time.

The enemy wants to slither into your decision-making process and get you to take advantage of God's grace. As a former angel, Satan knows as well as anyone that God exists and that he couldn't convince you there is a power greater than God. The enemy's plan of attack must be sneaky. He took the truth of Scripture and twisted it with Eve in the garden, and now he tries to twist our understanding of grace.

I have wrongly used the story of the adulterous woman from John 8:2–11 numerous times to excuse my sin. *God will forgive me just like He forgave the adulterous woman. It's okay.*

But then I remember what actually happened in that passage of Scripture.

> At dawn he appeared again in the temple courts, where all the people gathered around him, and he sat down to teach them. The teachers of the law and the Pharisees brought in a woman caught in adultery. They made her stand before the group and said to Jesus, "Teacher, this woman was caught in the act of adultery. In the Law Moses commanded us to stone such

women. Now what do you say?" They were using this question as a trap, in order to have a basis for accusing him.

But Jesus bent down and started to write on the ground with his finger. When they kept on questioning him, he straightened up and said to them, "Let any one of you who is without sin be the first to throw a stone at her." Again he stooped down and wrote on the ground.

At this, those who heard began to go away one at a time, the older ones first, until only Jesus was left, with the woman still standing there. Jesus straightened up and asked her, "Woman, where are they? Has no one condemned you?"

"No one, sir," she said.

"Then neither do I condemn you," Jesus declared. "Go now and leave your life of sin."

When Jesus talked about the sinless man throwing the first stone, He showed us that it's God's job, and His alone, to serve as Judge.

But there's more to this story. Jesus' words in the last verse of that passage are equally instructive when he tells the woman, "Go now and leave your life of sin."

Yes, God forgives you when you fall. He sees your biggest regrets and says, "Come back to Me, my child." He sees you gossiping about your coworker, and He know how far you went with that guy Friday night. Although He gives you grace, you must also listen to Him when he says, "Go away from your sin, my child."

I used to overlook that last verse. Now I understand it to be one of the most important parts of my walk with Christ.

God stands ready to grant forgiveness, but it takes more than being sorry if we want to receive it. You must confess your sins to be forgiven. Then you should heed Jesus' final words to the adulterous woman and strive not to commit your sins again.

Yes, God will forgive you if you fail again, but that's not a gift that should be abused.

Pray for wisdom and discernment each morning. Pray that you can hear Jesus' voice commanding you, "Go and leave your life of sin" and not the enemy's suggesting, "Go ahead and do what you want. God will forgive you. It'll be okay!"

Knowing God has forgiven you should lead you to respect and honor His word and strive to please Him. Being thankful for His grace should produce a change within you—a desire to live a life that reflects your belief in His saving power. And that's not just a power to save you from your sins, but also to save you from committing them again. If forgiveness doesn't cause you to want to change your ways, perhaps you should ask yourself how sorry you really are for your sins.

Let's revere God, okay? Let's not throw out meaningless apologies that lead to no actions. Let's obey Him because He is great and mighty. We should love Him in such a way that others cannot help but notice something different about our lives. Then when they ask why we are different, we can tell them how God's forgiveness has changed us.

Let's live lives that show we care about Him, that show we want to make Him proud, and that show we understand we've been forgiven even though we don't deserve to be.

Real Talk

- What is your forbidden fruit of choice?
- In what ways have you tried to take advantage of God's grace?
- How can you set the balance between accepting God's grace, realizing He does not call you to perfection, and still striving to walk in the light?
- What is your prayer for your walk with Christ? Let that be your prayer now.

Chapter 17

Carry the Cross

I studied abroad in Costa Rica for a mini-mester and made a dumb decision to book my flights separately. In order to get on my connecting flight home, I had to pick up my luggage at baggage claim, and then go back through the check-in process and security line all over again.

That kind of planning is just one reason why I'm writing this book instead of a travel guide.

During that hassle, I stepped onto an elevator occupied by a precious-looking family. The couple had two young boys and a double stroller. From what I could tell by the woman's clothing, the family was Muslim. The parents struggled getting the boys out of the elevator in their rush to wherever they were headed. One boy moved quickly while the other stared into space and needed to have his hand grabbed to be led out.

An older couple replaced the family in the elevator. The woman wore a beautiful diamond cross necklace around her neck and an I-want-to-speak-to-the-manager-immediately hairstyle.

"Make you think about our kids when they were babies?" the husband asked.

The wife glared back at him.

"No," she retorted. "Makes me think about how our country is getting run over by those kinds of people."

I was so shocked that I had to process what I had just witnessed. This "Christian" woman saw the parents and children not as a family, but as problems. She labeled them by their religion. Her husband saw the children and connected through the idea of family, something the two couples held in common—but the wife could only see how they were different. How she was better.

As the door opened and the couple left the elevator, I swiped my phone screen about five times to look busy. I couldn't believe that such hatred had come from a woman wearing a cross necklace. How could she act like she was better than that family?

The woman clearly should not have said those words. In fact, she should never have thought them. Based on what I heard, she appeared to have a heart issue. Our words are a reflection of our thoughts, and our thoughts reflect our hearts. What comes from our hearts forms our character, and our character influences our actions.

Matthew 16:24–26 is a convicting passage:

> Then Jesus told his disciples, "If anyone would come after me, let him deny himself and take up his cross and follow me. For whoever would save his life will lose it, but whoever loses his life for my sake will find it. For what will it profit a man if he gains the whole world and forfeits his soul? Or what shall a man give in return for his soul?" (ESV)

When we allow sinful and disheartening thoughts to drag us down, we are in danger of dropping our cross.

But here's the really convicting part. The "Christian" woman wasn't the only person who dropped her cross in that elevator.

As I was performing my needless phone swipes, I caught sight of the silver cross ring I wore on one of my fingers. There I was with my own Christian symbol, and I had not stood up for the Muslim family. I didn't remind the "Christian" woman that Jesus commands us to love one another. Instead, I had stared at my phone, unable to be bold for my faith while wearing my cross ring.

Take note sometime of how many jewelry stores sell the symbol of Christianity and how many celebrities wear the cross. The cross should never be just a fashion statement. The cross should be a reminder of the pain and agony Jesus suffered. For him, the cross wasn't a 13-carat diamond meant to be noticed. It was the ultimate form of cruel death.

In the airport elevator, I had forgotten to represent the cross. I should have boldly told the woman, "Those are people and deserve to be treated as such." I should have said something about love and that the Creator we both worship had created that family too. I hadn't forgotten about the cross when I was looking for a piece of jewelry to match my sweater, but I had forgotten to carry it onto the elevator.

We have opportunities to carry our crosses every day. Are you taking advantage of the chances you receive to spread the gospel? Are you living a bold life that proclaims love? Or are you treating your relationship with Christ as a fashion statement—when it's suddenly awkward and not "in season," you choose to remain silent and stay hidden? The cross is a symbol of Christianity because of the bold statement Jesus made on it. If you're going to wear that symbol, carry it well.

Real Talk

- If you would have been me on that elevator, would you have said anything to the woman? If so, what?
- What is the difference between wearing a cross and carrying your cross?
- What prevents you from being more bold in your faith?
- What steps can you take to be more bold in your faith?
- Pray for courage so that you can be a good representative of Christianity.

Chapter 18

Be Holy

I'm not afraid to try new things. Before my senior year of college, I worked at a new church in Florida. A good friend and fellow intern—almost like a younger brother to me—asked if I wanted to swing dance. I said I'd give it a try.

I had never swing danced before. We have two-stepping in Texas, but I wasn't too hot at that dance. So I was a little apprehensive about what I was getting myself into. The best part came at the end, when my friend flipped me. I twirled, he put his arm around my back, lifted me up, flipped me over while holding my back, and I landed on two feet. I felt like Simone Biles on the Olympic floor exercise. (I'm not saying my air time *looked* like Simone's, just that I *felt* like her.)

The flip brought oohs and aahs from the girls watching, and my friend offered to flip anyone who was interested. But none of the girls wanted to.

"I'll be flipped again," I said.

"I can't flip you again," he said. "I'm sorry."

I thought he was joking. I was all ready to give it another go, especially since no one else was willing.

But my friend was serious. He said he had a girlfriend, and out of respect for her, he would not flip anyone more than once without checking with her first. He knew she would be fine with one flip, but to flip the same girl twice—and who knows, maybe more times—could potentially upset her. He had drawn a line at one flip, and he wouldn't cross it.

My friend had an awareness of others that many do not. As far as I could tell, he was having fun and would have liked to do more flips. And because I now had one flip of experience on my dancing résumé, the next one surely would be better. But he was in a good relationship, and he didn't want to do anything that could possibly make his girlfriend unhappy. His happiness in that moment was trumped by the happiness of his girlfriend.

That's an impressive guy.

Let's apply his awareness to our relationship with God.

I think sometimes we get so caught up in our own happiness that we lose concern about what makes the One we serve happy.

One more drink. Thirty more minutes of time spent in front of the mirror. One more date with the wrong guy. We can make those decisions without first considering what God thinks about them and how they affect our relationship with Him.

God calls us to be holy. What does that mean, anyway? Well, the definition of *holy* is "to be set apart." Why does God call us to be holy? Because He is holy.

> Therefore, with minds that are alert and fully sober, set your hope on the grace to be brought to you when Jesus Christ is revealed at his coming. As obedient children, do not conform

to the evil desires you had when you lived in ignorance. But just as he who called you is holy, so be holy in all you do; for it is written: "Be holy, because I am holy." (1 Peter 1:13–16)

God is apart—or separate—from His creation because of His perfect nature. But God also created us to be in relationship with Him. Adam and Eve's decision in the garden introduced sin into God's creation. Sin made us unholy, and God is holy. In order to have relationship with us, He called us to be holy.

In the Old Testament, people had to observe the laws of the old covenant in order to be holy and enjoy a relationship with God. In the New Testament, Jesus' sacrificial death replaced all the rules and laws that bridged the gap between God's holiness and our unholiness.

We are still part of this world, but at the same time, God has called us to be "set apart" for Him. "In the world, but not of the world," is one way that's often stated. Because we are in relationship with Him, we need to consider whether our words, thoughts, and actions are pleasing to Him. Are we choosing to participate in unholy activities while trying to maintain relationship with a holy God?

Let's commit to honoring our relationship with God in the same manner that my friend the flipper honored his girlfriend. That means being serious about honoring God and being on alert against unholy activities that prevent us from living the life He wants for us.

Real Talk

- What would it look like for you to be "set apart" at your job, at your school, or while hanging out with your friends?
- Over the next twenty-four hours, what is one thing you could do outside of your normal routine that would honor God?
- How would your weekend plans change if you were to bounce them off Jesus to see what He thinks about them?
- Pray and ask forgiveness for the decisions you've made that didn't please God. Commit to always taking His desires into account in future decisions.

LIE #7

Strong women cry only in the bathroom.

Chapter 19

The Proper Foundation

I have a history of fainting because of low blood sugar—sometimes at really embarrassing moments.

One time was on a fifth-grade field trip. Another time, I fainted on a subway in a foreign country. Talk about great timing. And then there was the episode in the middle of a flight when I was eighteen and going to my brother's college graduation.

At least my body gives me about a two-minute warning before I faint. Black clouds fill my vision. My heart races. And then it's lights out.

When black clouds appeared on that flight, for some reason the idea of fainting in the bathroom sounded better than at my seat. I started making my way down the aisle when the flight attendant stopped me.

"Young lady," she said, "you need to return to your seat. The fasten seat belt light is on."

I replied by fainting into her arms. Oops.

The next thing I knew, doctors on the flight were asking if I was diabetic. Either they were yelling or I was hypersensitive to sound as I came to. Either way, the commotion certainly didn't draw any attention *away* from me.

"No, opposite," I told the doctors. "I need sugar."

I was fine within about five minutes. However, just as I'd feared, everybody in the cabin kept looking at me. I think some were freaking out. They might have been even in worse shape than me by that point!

But no kidding, they had a *stretcher* waiting for me at our destination.

I don't think it would have been much worse if a gate agent had announced: "Your attention please. For those of you who were not on this flight, Grace fainted. She'll be rolling past you on a stretcher any second now if you want to see who I'm talking about."

How embarrassing.

Later on, my mom scolded me for leaving my seat. "You cannot just go to the bathroom when you have to faint," she said. "You could hit your head. You cannot hide from everyone. We want to help."

Mom was right, as usual. That was not one of my better decisions. But I tend to want to run and hide to save face instead of fainting in front of people. I think I can handle things myself—until I wake up in the aisle of an airplane with what seems like fifty wide-open eyes staring down at me.

Hide and Seek

Fainting spells aren't the only time I hide. I tend to hide my emotions, as well. And, like many young ladies, I run to the bathroom when I suffer heartbreak.

I remember the first time I locked myself in the bathroom of a crowded get-together. The guy I thought I was dating hooked up with someone else. I tried to hide my hurt, to pretend that everything was just fine. I desperately wanted to act like our relationship was great and that I was as happy as could be.

I couldn't pull it off, so I escaped to the bathroom. In the mirror, I saw tears making an all-out sprint down my face—taking my mascara with them. All I could do was look at my reflection and try to figure out what more I could have done so that guy would have stayed with me instead of making a random hook-up. *What was so wrong with me,* I wondered, *that no guy wants to stay with me?*

Do you know what that feels like? Have you also been that girl who locked herself in a bathroom or bedroom to hide her emotions?

I've learned through difficult experiences that guys who break your heart and don't realize how great you are—they aren't worth your time. As I've said before, our worth comes from our Creator. He's taught me that embracing His love is more important than any guy. He has also taught me there are better places to cry than all alone in a bathroom. I can run to Him to cry. I have friends and family ready to listen, and He's placed me in a church community that would support me if I'd only ask.

One of the most important things I've learned through heartbreaks is to wait for a man who puts Christ first and loves me like Christ loves me.

We're more than halfway through refuting the ten lies listed in the first chapter of this book. Those are lies of Satan intended to make us doubt our worth. I don't know if, like me, you have this image of Satan dressed in red with a pointy tail, a sharp beard, and a pitchfork, clearly out to make us feel unworthy of God's love. But sometimes the one who causes us girls to question our worth has great hair, warm eyes, and bulging biceps. He's usually not trying to make us doubt ourselves as much as he is trying to boost his own self-image. But without uttering a single word—or even looking in our direction—he can send us into the depths of doubt by denying us or cheating on us.

I mistakenly let that one guy determine my value, and he failed me. Humans tend to do that. I chose to dance with him and followed his lead instead of the Lord's—and his lead ran me right into the bathroom to talk to the puffy-eyed girl in the mirror.

Yes, it was the guy's fault for choosing to hook up with another girl, but it was my mistake for allowing his actions to knock down my self-worth.

Shelter in the Storm

If this story sounds remotely familiar to you, I want you to read the following passage of Scripture—aloud. Read it like you would imagine God saying this to you when you're crying in the bathroom.

> Why do you call me "Lord, Lord," and not do what I tell you? Everyone who comes to me and hears my words and does them, I will show you what he is like: he is like a man building a house, who dug deep and laid the foundation on the rock. And when a flood arose, the stream broke against that house and could not shake it, because it had been well built. But the one who hears and does not do them is like a man who built a house on the ground without a foundation. When the stream broke against it, immediately it fell, and the ruin of that house was great. (Luke 6:46–49, ESV)

I vividly remember reading this exact passage after that particular heartbreak. I was locked in my bedroom, not wanting anyone to hear me bawl over a guy who didn't care about me as much as I hoped.

As I read, it was like God asked me, "Grace, why did you put your worth in the hands of a guy? Why was *he* your foundation?"

I shouted my reply in my thoughts: *But he was hot, God! He made me feel wanted!*

I had been going through a bad stage of insecurity. Then when I met that guy, I realized that maybe, just maybe, I *was* lovable after all. Maybe I had the ability to be good enough for a good-looking, popular guy. Maybe I could be considered desirable by someone who met the world's definition of "cool." I falsely believed that he could bring me something I really needed at that point in my life: hope.

Then all those dreams came crashing in on me, and I realized I was even more heartbroken than before. A storm came, and the foundation I had built on that guy wasn't strong enough to protect me from the pain, loneliness, and hurt of my broken heart. Actually, as I reached a point where I could look back on the experience without raw emotions, I realized that building my foundation on that guy *was* my storm. I had placed my worth on a landfill, and it began rotting me to the core.

The Lord used that storm to break me and crumble my dreams in order to remind me that He should be my foundation. I needed to rebuild my life on Him. I learned the hard way that a guy can't be my rock, no matter how good looking or popular he is. I had thought otherwise, and the waters swept away my joy.

Only God is strong enough to be our Rock. A guy can give us compliments every day; God gives us new mercies every day. I'm thankful that I now understand which one is more meaningful.

Real Talk

- Where is your favorite place to run when you want to hide?
- Do you have a habit of building your foundation on guys?
- If you are currently in a relationship, are you building your foundation on that guy?
- How can you make Christ your foundation instead of guys?
- Pray and ask God to reveal to you areas of your life where you've built your foundation on someone or something other than Him.

Chapter 20

What to Do with a Broken Heart

*I*f you've never experienced heartbreak, raise your hand. I don't need to be able to see you to assume that no hands are raised. I wish I could tell you the guy in the previous chapter is the only one who broke my heart. My, how I wish I could tell you that. But I can't.

Maybe you experienced heartbreak through a breakup, or maybe you didn't get your dream job. Maybe one of your parents left you when you were young and you still struggle to cope with the heartache that developed from the night that car drove away. Whether your heartbreak stems from a parent, boy, or boss, I pray you read these five truths I've learned through heartbreak and hold onto them when you have a broken heart.

1. God wants you to cry to Him.

Let's kick things off right with this verse, Psalm 145:18: "The LORD is near to all who call on him, to all who call on him in truth."

I've felt guilty in the past for going to God with work drama, my guy drama, and for telling Him how I felt when relationships ended or I got dumped. That's an unwarranted guilt. God already knows your thoughts, so you might as well express them to Him. Telling Him how you feel can be part of your healing process. Often it's the first step.

God knows how sensitive you are, whether you enjoy talking about your feelings, or whether you pretend not to be in pain when your heart breaks. He also knows your future and wants you to bring your pain and worries to Him, so He can give you hope for the future He has planned for you.

Stop hiding your emotions and pretending you're fine. It's okay to hurt when you don't get the job you applied for. It's okay to hurt when a relationship doesn't turn out as you'd hoped. It's also okay to not be okay. You can't get back to okay, though, until you first admit you've been hurt.

When your heart breaks, ask God if you can cry on His shoulders. Think about this: if He has a great future planned for you, wouldn't He want to take care of you in the present?

2. God created community for times such as heartbreaks.

God has placed you among people to whom you can cry out. Choose wisely, though. Lean on friends who you trust and who are mature in their faith. Seek help from pastors or church leaders. Even if you are not comfortable going to a pastor or leader for help, they can guide you to someone capable of walking with you through your pain.

This is very important: do not pour your heart out to a member of the opposite sex unless there is built-in accountability for both of you. Even then, be extremely careful. No boy should ever be treated as though he is your husband. This isn't just about your physical relationship. This boundary also carries over to your emotional relationship. Even if you think he is helping you, please remember that he is *not* your husband. You should not be connecting with him on a husband-like level. You are in a vulnerable place after heartbreak. Establish accountability. Please, follow this advice.

The bottom line is that God can speak through those who love and serve Him. He can bring you peace and comfort through them. Allow those He has placed around you to help when you have fallen. If you feel like you're losing your battle, believers who have made it through heartbreak like yours can remind you that Christ has already won on your behalf.

3. Anyone or anything that breaks your heart doesn't deserve your heart.

When a guy causes you to cry from heartbreak, breathe in, breathe out. Do it again if you need to. And again. And again. When your boss says you are laid off, walk out the door and trust that God's plan is better. When you face any rejection, trust the Author of your story to use your trial to become a testimony.

If God's plan is for you to marry, have faith that one day—yeah, I know, the dreaded "one day"—you will find a guy who loves you with the love of Jesus. You *will* find a man who appreciates you and understands how precious your heart is. Remember, people take better care of those things they consider precious.

If you thought God's plan was for you to work at your dream company, yet you received a voicemail starting with, "I'm sorry, but . . ."—trust Him. Once again, the closed door could be God whispering, "You'll see one day." Trust for the dreaded one day. Closed doors and heartbreak can lead us where we were called to be all along.

4. The only one who can satisfy the human heart is the One who created it.

God knows your heart better than anyone. That's the advantage of creating you! Because He created your heart, He knows better than anyone how to repair your broken heart. When your heart's broken, give it to Him. He knows what to do with it.

5. One relationship matters more than all others.

Feeling wanted is amazing. Being chosen is better.

God sees all your flaws and loves you anyway. In fact, He chose you to be a daughter of the King of kings. What relationship could be better than that?

I am a daughter of the One who created everything good, including chocolate, red roses, and laughter. He is in control, and he hears the cries of my broken heart—even when I'm hiding behind a locked door.

God's love is greater than anyone who breaks my heart. It's more beautiful than the star quarterback who can make a football-hating woman stop flipping channels and watch a game.

Because of God's love, I've learned it really doesn't matter what the guys who break my heart think about me. (Or don't think about me.) It doesn't matter if my boss is not the nicest to me. It doesn't matter if I don't get a text back from the guy I was crushing on. It doesn't matter if the man I think is the love of my life cheats on me. The only thing that matters is living a life that celebrates the love God has given me.

We worship the greatest source of love—someone we can cry to and who takes our tears of heartache and uses them for His glory.

The painful truth is that as long as you take the risk of entering into relationships, you will experience some type of heartbreak. It can be a hot guy or a friend or a family member. Heartbreak can come in a variety of ways, and often unexpectedly.

But remember: just because your heart is broken doesn't mean *you* are broken. God knitted you together in your mother's womb and handcrafted your heart. You were planned since the beginning—yes, the "In the beginning" of Genesis 1:1 beginning. Before that, actually.

God didn't create us and say, "Good luck—see you down the road." He created us for relationship with Him. He is jealous of anything that comes between you and a relationship with Him. God, jealous of something? If it's preventing you from dancing with Him, then yes.

Allow me to repeat a question about God that I asked you to consider earlier in this chapter: if He has a great future planned for you, wouldn't He want to take care of you in the present?

Of course He does!

You can't lock a door that will prevent Him from bringing His peace to you. You can't deliver an Oscar-winning "everything's fine" acting job that fools Him. You can't hide your emotions in a place where His comfort can't find you.

You can't have a heart so broken that He can't restore it.

So give your broken heart to Him.

Real Talk

- How many times would you estimate you've had your heart broken?
- When was your last broken heart? How long did it take to heal—or is it still healing?
- Write a personal, heartfelt prayer to God. Tell Him your worries and fears. If your heart is broken, tell Him why. Be completely honest with yourself and with God.

Chapter 21

Uncommon Strength

*E*lizabeth Vinturella is one of the sweetest ladies I know.

You might know a woman who just by being in her presence gives you peace, a mother's love, and the grace of God. The enemy fears her smile.

That's "Mrs. Liz" for me, and I want what she has: joy that comes directly from the Lord.

Mrs. Liz has learned to smile through pain.

In 2011, Mrs. Liz heard these words: "There's been a boat crash, and we don't know where Sam is."

Samantha was Mrs. Liz's twelve-year-old daughter. Sam had been on a family boat outing near Shell Beach in Louisiana. Their boat collided with another, and Sam, her sister, and two cousins were thrown into the water. All but Sam were rescued. Three days later, Sam's body was found.

Sam had this incredibly bright smile and outgoing personality. She was cherished by every member of our church family. Sam loved the Lord and making others laugh.

We like to say "God gives us joy in suffering." But as I've tried to imagine what it must have been like for Mrs. Liz to bury her twelve-year-old daughter—to know that Sam would never have another theater performance, never go to prom, and no longer grace our church with that infectious smile—the thought of God giving us joy in suffering seems too difficult to comprehend.

I asked Mrs. Liz how she made it through the loss of Sam. She described the first holiday without her daughter. Her family was traveling and she wondered: *How am I going to get through this week? How am I going to get through this month? How am I going to get through the day Sam's friends start high school, go to their first prom, graduate, and decorate their dorm rooms?*

Mrs. Liz shared her pain with a friend who gave her this advice: "Liz, just do today."

I don't know about you, but I'm relieved that God doesn't call us to plan how we will get through next year. He doesn't call us to wonder how we'll survive another heartbreak. Or the next holiday without a loved one. He calls us to trust that He can give us joy in suffering. To allow Him to turn our trials into testimonies of His strength.

But God tells us, "Just do today—with Me."

Mrs. Liz is one of the strongest women I know. She started a ministry and a blog (justdotoday.org) that help others experiencing trials similar to her loss of Sam. Mrs. Liz got hit by an excruciatingly painful situation, and she gave it to God.

Dancing in the Rain

Anna and I were co-counselors at a summer camp. Every morning, Anna would shout to the campers, with music blaring, "It is gonna be the best day ever!"

I'm all for positivity, but at 6:30 a.m. that wasn't always the best wake-up call. Still, Anna's enthusiasm for what was to come pumped up the campers. She made the rest of the day worth getting out of bed for. Even at 6:30.

Joyful, positive, uplifting Anna faced her fair share of trials in life. Four of her friends died in a car accident during her sophomore year of college. The following summer, Anna described for me the intensity of the pain she had to endure.

"What was hard was," she said, then paused, "it wasn't 'well with my soul.' I didn't shower. I didn't want to go to school on some days. I began to wonder, 'Why not me? Why am I here?'"

One day amid the continued suffering, a mentor gently told Anna, "You're going to have to learn to dance in the rain."

In other words, at some point during her healing process, Anna would have to discover the joy in her suffering. She would have to learn not just how to move on, but how to have joy in the present despite the pain of the past. She would have to trust God.

Each day brought challenges for Anna, but she held on to the truth that her Savior loved her, cared about her, and had greater plans for her than she could ever dream.

I later watched Anna do something beautiful. Anna was program director at our summer camp, and one day it rained. She didn't usually celebrate rain. Rain tended to ruin her planned activities. But on this day, Anna looked at me, and then without even grabbing her raincoat, began to dance in the rain with about thirty-five campers of various ages. In that moment, she taught thirty-five campers that rain didn't mean their day was ruined and they had to forfeit their joy. In fact, joy was what gave Anna the momentum to dance in the rain.

Was rain what Anna wanted? No. But did God use the rain for His glory? Yes.

It would be ridiculous to say that death is a good thing. Death and pain are the result of the fall—the day humanity invited evil to enter into God's creation. One of the many cool things about God, though, is how He uses every opportunity—whether good or evil—to proclaim His kingdom. We serve a God who doesn't promise painless lives, but instead promises that if we trust Him, He will bring joy for our mornings.

If someone has led you to believe that joy means life is great, no one will be ill, and the sun is always shining, that is incorrect. I used to believe that my soul's peace depended on my circumstances. Now, I am learning that my soul's peace depends on the One who created my soul. I used to believe that my level of joy depended on my level of happiness. I am learning that joy can exist without happiness.

The world tries to sell us happiness. I'm all for feeling happy, but happiness is dependent upon circumstances, which are ever-changing. Joy doesn't depend on circumstances. It isn't measured by the number of times we have pleasant experiences. It's a fruit of the Spirit, and a gift from God. Joy doesn't mean we don't cry; it simply means that even through the pain and tears, the Lord is faithful and we understand that His good is the ultimate good.

Some of the most joyful people I know have experienced the worst aspects of life, yet they held onto God's promise and learned to dance in the rain. They don't necessarily know how they will survive the next year or month or week, but they have learned to focus on just doing today.

You will go through seasons of life where you want to shake your fist and scream at God, "It is not well with my soul!" Life hurts sometimes. Disease appears to be ruining us. Death looks to be winning when it steals our friends and family members. Fortunately, we serve a God who brings rainbows after rain, turns trials into testimonies, and uses confusing situations to build our trust in Him.

Before I close this chapter, I want to make this admission: if you are looking for a profound explanation of why bad things happen to the best people, I can't provide it. What I can tell you, though, is that the Lord provides strength even in the worst of trials.

That's where trust enters the scene.

It's interesting to see friends reach moments in their lives when they realize that they're not God. I've done that. Our failures remind us that we aren't God. Life not going the way we planned reminds us of this too. We don't hold the ultimate power. God does. We don't know what will happen tomorrow or next week or five years from now. God does, so we should choose to trust Him.

He doesn't ask much more of us than to trust Him to provide the strength we need—whether it's for the next five years, for tomorrow, or just to do today.

Real Talk

- Have you ever felt that it is not "well with my soul"?
- How can you combat that feeling?
- Name one person who has the type of joy you want to have. What would it take for you to have that joy?
- Pray for your soul to be filled with joy. Ask God to turn your trials into testimonies.

Lie #8

Nicholas Sparks writes the best love stories.

Chapter 22

Crushing It!

*W*hat type of guy do you think is worth crushing on?

I have to laugh as I look back at the progression of my crushes.

My first came at twelve: Zac Efron. The moment I looked into his blue eyes as he sang "Start of Something New" on *High School Musical*, I knew he was the one. (Little-known fact: he was actually singing that song to me, not Gabriella.) With his shaggy brown hair, nice biceps, and that voice, Zac captured my attention. I knew right then I would end up either with Zac or a guy just like him. I wouldn't settle for anyone mediocre-looking from that point on. Zac set the standard.

In high school, sports became the biggest factor. Any guy wearing a sports uniform was attractive. If he played basketball and had brown eyes, I was sold. If he played football—done deal.

Transitioning from high school to college, I was all about the dad bod on an overly confident frat boy who drove a nice car. I still can't explain why it became a thing to have a guy whose body revealed that while he went to the gym occasionally, he also didn't hesitate to eat an extra slice of pizza. Regardless of the reason, I went through that period knowing without a doubt that "the one" would be an outgoing guy who wore top-tier frat letters.

Trends and fads change what we consider attractive.

Even recently a friend asked what I wanted my husband to look like. Without thinking, I blurted, "I have no clue, but he better be attractive!"

Actually, if I had taken just a second before responding, I would have said six-foot-two with brown hair and, preferably, a six-pack. He'd have a crazy cool job that would allow me to share in the perks and us to be financially stable for life.

For most of my life, I've allowed myself to admire men for their looks and possessions. Even now, too often, that is how I define attractive. I strive every day to pray for the Lord's eyes—to see how He sees. (Once again, I don't have everything figured out. But I'm trying.)

But the answer to my friend's question revealed that I've always dreamed of the type of guy that other girls would fall for—the type of guy that would cause other girls to envy me.

Setting Standards

That realization isn't easy to swallow. Through the years, as the traits I've looked for in a guy have changed, I've set my standards by listening to what the world says is attractive rather than what my heart says.

But now I know. I know that looks fade and if I keep chasing after boys who are hot, I am simply wasting my time and emotions, and I'm almost guaranteed to end up crying again over a boy who didn't love me like Jesus. It took me a while to realize my physical appearance didn't determine my worth, but it took me even longer to realize that men's physical appearance also didn't determine their worth.

My heart knows what I should find attractive. A guy who smiles a lot, loves well, prays a prayer of thanks before the meal, and tips the waiter well because he wants to be a blessing. Even better, being in his presence makes those around him feel the love of Christ. He's attractive because he makes you belly-laugh and want to dance even when there's no music—all while challenging you every day to grow into the woman God created you to be.

Hollywood fame, football jersey, or fraternity label aren't factors. He might not be a good-looking doctor or earn a million bucks a year. He doesn't need to have a six-pack, perfect tan, or blue eyes.

I want the guy I ultimately fall in love with to look like Jesus as much as any of us can. I used to think I wanted to marry a guy whose arms show how much he's been lifting at the gym. Now, I want a guy whose arms are reaching out to help others. If his legs aren't perfectly toned, that's fine as long as they are willing go where the Lord leads them. Eye color doesn't matter. It does matter whether his eyes look for the good in others instead of the attractive things of this world. His words should be filled with compassion, loving all people, and never used for destruction.

He'll be patient—not pushing my boundaries, admiring my desire for purity until marriage, and seeking the same for himself.

He'll be the same guy on Friday night that he is in church on Sunday morning. The tears he'll make me cry will be tears of joy. When he makes a mistake, he'll admit it and ask for forgiveness. When I make a mistake and admit it, he'll give grace.

His bursting love for the Creator will cause all those who know him to want to accept Christ as their Savior. Instead of fitting my old definitions of attractive—definitions that would wind up coming between God and me—he will lead me into a closer relationship with Christ.

It won't even matter if he can't afford a rock for my ring finger, because He's placed His foundation on the Rock.

That's a lengthy list! But we need to be looking for a lot in a guy. It bothers me to see friends who "settle" in choosing a guy. They pick a guy who doesn't treat them in a manner they deserve. They go for a guy who looks good but doesn't respect them, and they wind up wasting tears on guys who don't deserve their time.

I've certainly crushed on my fair share of guys who weren't worth my time. It wasn't until recently that I've realized the importance of crushing on someone who crushes on God.

While working at a summer camp, I had a crush on a fellow counselor. Let's call him David. We set up a lunch date.

This was three months after a bad experience with a guy at a date function in college. (A date function doesn't mean you're dating, but it usually means you are at least interested in possibly dating that person.)

This guy had seemed really into me when he asked me to the date function, and butterflies circled inside my stomach each time he talked to me. We had been flirting, talking, or whatever you want to call the "we kinda like each other" phase.

During the function, he told me how much he respected my beliefs.

"I respect who you are and your desire to wait," he told me. "Your writing is a gift, and you are going places."

The next morning, I was so excited about the possibilities with this guy. He was so nice and fun. Until I walked in on him sleeping with another girl. I guess he realized I wouldn't give him what he wanted, so he found someone who would.

Right then, I felt as wanted as a fruit cup at McDonald's. Nobody goes to McDonald's because they want fruit, right? Just like, I assumed, no one goes on a date function wanting the Christian girl. I was Grace Valentine, fruit cup.

That experience was still fresh in my memory on the lunch date with the camp counselor. That date was the exact opposite of the date function. David prayed before we ate and talked about God like a personal friend instead of an authority figure. He wanted to hear what God was doing in my life. He was kind, he cared, and he loved Jesus. And he didn't pressure me to even hug him good-bye! He showed nothing but respect for me as a woman. His words matched his actions.

Honestly, I felt a little out of place during that lunch. But I had fun. He was charming, sweet, and hilarious, and he made me feel wanted and appreciated. I was giddy for David. And honestly, his personality was worth more than any six-pack.

The way David treated me was a new experience I wasn't prepared for. It felt weird in some ways. But it also felt right, like this was an important date for me to have.

I didn't end up with that guy. Camp ended and we went back to our separate lives. But I think God used that lunch to remind me how a guy worth crushing on looks, acts, and talks.

David didn't place a checkmark in many of my old boxes. He wasn't in a top-tier fraternity. He wasn't famous. I had no idea if he could sing well. He didn't have a six-pack or play football. I couldn't tell you for sure, but I didn't see any evidence he had a lot of money.

The point was clear: I could meet guys who check few of my boxes but turn out to be even better than what I was looking for. I could meet a child of the King who lived his life in a way that pleases God.

Loved Well

As I've compared those two dating experiences, I've thought about one thing the guys had in common: they were nice. Even the one who slept with the other girl was nice to me. (Hey, even the girl who slept with him was nice.)

The problem with that whole date function situation, however, was me.

I should not have been crushing on a guy like him. We obviously were in different places in our lives. I crushed on him because he was funny, cool, and cute. Those are great traits, and ones I want in my future husband. But he wasn't pursuing Christ the same as I was.

The camp counselor was, and although we didn't wind up having a cool hashtag wedding, I learned a valuable lesson through him: the guys who crush on Jesus are the ones to crush on. The guys who crush on Jesus are, honestly, more fun. We need to date men we can picture leading us in marriage—men who put Christ first, help us stay pure until marriage, and love us the same way the Lord does.

Let's revisit the topic of settling. I think we ladies tend to settle because we don't give ourselves enough credit. We settle because we don't allow ourselves to believe we deserve better.

My friend, you are a creation of God, and you are worthy of

a lifetime of adventure and love. You deserve someone who will encourage you in deeper ways than a "goodnight babe" text. You deserve someone who will make you belly-laugh and dance with no music. You deserve someone in whom you see joy, love, and leadership. You deserve someone who challenges you to grow as a friend and disciple. You deserve a guy who sees you chasing after the Lord and instead of stopping you, runs alongside you so that you are pursuing Christ together.

You are beautiful in God's eyes and worthy to be loved well. God treats you that way, and you deserve a man who wants to love you like God does.

In 1 Corinthians 13—the "Love Chapter"—verse 4 through the first part of verse 8 gives a beautiful description of love as designed by God:

> Love is patient, love is kind. It does not envy, it does not boast, it is not proud. It does not dishonor others, it is not self-seeking, it is not easily angered, it keeps no record of wrongs. Love does not delight in evil but rejoices with the truth. It always protects, always trusts, always hopes, always perseveres. Love never fails.

If you want to see how a guy measures up to what God says you deserve, see if you can truthfully place his name with each description. "Jon is patient, Jon is kind. Jon does not envy, Jon does not boast," and so on.

If you cannot honestly place a guy's name with those traits, you aren't being loved the way you deserve.

Now, here's a tougher question: can your name fit in those same slots?

While you're busy waiting for a man rooted in faith, remember that you need to be a woman of Christ. You need to be the type of woman who attracts the type of guy you want to be attracted to. But don't do so just to get a good guy. Do it because you have a God who has given everything for you and you know there is nothing greater to strive for than a life that loves the Creator of love itself.

God writes the best love stories, so don't pursue anything less than what He has planned for you. And by all means, don't settle for less, either.

To all the girls who have boyfriends who crush on Jesus and genuinely love them, I pray that you will maintain a relationship that reflects the love of our Savior. Always remember that even if the guy is great and faithful, you need your Savior more than you need him. Let your relationship be one in which you chase Jesus together. Both of you should be dancing with Him daily.

And to the girls like me who struggle with giving too much priority to a guy's physical attraction, I pray you soon realize that looks fade with age. If he can't make you smile, laugh, and feel challenged to be a better person now, then you won't be happy for a lifetime. God has someone faithful in store for you if you let Him write your love story instead of trying to write it yourself.

Just stop thinking that kind of guy is out of your league. God would disagree.

Regardless of how many jerks you've dated and how many mistakes you have made, you are worthy of respect, true love, and a gentleman who places God first in his life.

Pray and wait patiently for him, because he is the type of guy to crush on.

In the meantime, crush on God. Let Him show you His love. Let Him grasp your hand tightly and dance with you. Get used to the love given to you by the One who created you, and don't settle until you find a guy who wants to love you with that same type of love.

Trust God for His timing, and you'll be amazed at how your love story turns out.

Real Talk

- What are three characteristics you want in your future husband?
- To you, what kind of guy is worth crushing on?
- How can the Holy Spirit mold you into a woman of faith worth crushing on?
- Write a prayer asking God to help you notice which guys are worth crushing on.

Chapter 23

Remembering My First Love

H ave you ever been in love?" my best friend, Britta, asked.

Her question made me think back to the first guy I kissed. He once let me drive his truck. In south Louisiana, that's a pretty big deal. But it still isn't love.

There was the one guy I dated who told me I was hot and bought me sushi. Pretty serious stuff. But he's also the one who caused me to lock myself in the bathroom and cry. Although at one point I thought I could love him, I soon realized it was not love. So, no to him.

Then I thought of the one who is always there for me, makes me feel warm and fuzzy, and never fails to bring a smile to my face—the one I'm dying to see at the end of a long day. Chick-fil-A is awesome, but that wasn't the answer Britta was looking for.

After contemplating the question for what seemed like two minutes, I conceded the pathetic answer.

"Nope."

In that moment, I wondered what it's like to feel loved and

how it feels to look at a guy and think, *I could spend the rest of my life with you.* Sure, I'd had butterflies, been on dates, and thought I was close to being in love. There were guys I really liked, and I suffered heartbreak when they walked away. I had even created wedding hashtags in my mind for the guy I made sure to cross paths with every morning walking to my 10:15 class. (Yeah, he has no idea who I am . . .)

But I had never been in love.

Why not? I wondered. *Was I doing something wrong? Why didn't I have a Hallmark Channel love story and a guy who would look at me and say, "I love you—everything about you"?*

Am I not good enough to be loved?

Married to Jesus

As I write this, I am a senior at Baylor University—a noted "ring by spring" school. Fifteen members of my sorority got engaged before graduation. Girls come to school here expecting to end up with a spouse, and seven years later they bring tiny Tina and baby Ben—decked out in green and gold—back to the homecoming football game.

I thought I'd found the guy who would make that happen for me. I was a junior and found a guy who loved the Lord. He loved his mom, he seemed to be a great friend, and he definitely was interested in me. We talked every day, and he'd tell me how pretty I was.

We talked about going out on an official date, and I did the whole, "I have a good feeling about this" thing.

Then he lost interest in me, and the talk of going out on a date ended. Another "talking" fling faded out.

As much as I tried to pretend that dating at my age was not for me because "I'm focused on my career," that wasn't true. I wanted to fall in love like in the movies, complete with my Princess Mia from *Princess Diaries* moment when my foot popped while kissing a good-looking guy. I wanted to be like my friends and get my ring by spring.

And here I was already writing the sequel to my amazing love story when the first book fell apart somewhere around the middle of the second chapter.

The guy losing interest in me was not supposed to happen— that's not the way I'd scripted it.

Finally, after three confusing months of "What are we?" I realized it wasn't meant to be. I had to do something with my disappointment, so I went to ever-loyal and faithful Chick-fil-A for some needed me-time, which wound up becoming mad-at-God time. I opened up and told God how I felt.

Wasn't it weird that I'd never been in love? Why, according to my research, was I the only Christian twentysomething in the world who didn't have a serious boyfriend? Or a fiancé? Was I not loveable? I could plot a good love story for myself, but why wouldn't the Lord cowrite it with me? Why couldn't He just give me the love of my life?

As has happened often when I ask God those types of questions, I sensed Him whispering a response into my heart: *Grace. Do you not see me here? I have been here the whole time!*

My next thought came immediately: *But God, you don't count!*

I honestly thought that, right there in Chick-fil-A. Then I caught myself wondering, *Why did I think that God's love didn't count as "the love of my life"?*

I run away from cheesy Christian lines, like "I don't need a man—I'm married to Jesus!" Those lines have always annoyed me. It's not that easy to accept my lack of a love life and claim that Jesus can fully satisfy my need for love and affection. Jesus loves me. I get that. But there's still something missing in my love column. Jesus does a lot of things for me, but I also need someone to tell me I'm beautiful and reach over and touch me on the leg while he's driving us to a movie.

This time, however, I felt my heart being tugged to realize that there just might be a bit of truth in that married-to-Jesus line.

First Love

My friend Sarah once told me she was going back to her "first love." And at first, I was about to puke. I hoped she wasn't talking about that guy she dated in high school. I strongly disliked him. I thought of SoccerBaller94 from her AIM chat back in middle school. *Please, do not be him.*

While I tried to place a name on whom Sarah was talking about, she described her first love as someone who had sacrificed everything for her. He had put her first, pursued her every morning, and never failed to bring her joy.

She was talking about Jesus. At first, I laughed to myself at how cheesy that sounded. But as her words sank in, I stopped laughing. That's the answer I knew all along was correct. It *is* cheesy, but it's what I learned after my I-won't-have-a-serious-boyfriend-out-of-college crisis during my junior year.

Sometimes I wonder if Jesus' love is out of my league. But no—Jesus made it possible for me when He stretched His arms to be nailed to a cross so that all of us can have eternal freedom in Him. While we can get so fixated on finding a love from this world, what Jesus did on the cross continues to pour out His love for us.

> I pray that out of his glorious riches he may strengthen you with power through his Spirit in your inner being, so that Christ may dwell in your hearts through faith. And I pray that you, being rooted and established in love, may have power, together with all the Lord's holy people, to grasp how wide and long and high and deep is the love of Christ. (Ephesians 3:16–18)

How I wish I could talk about this over ice cream with each one of you, because much of what we're talking about in this book becomes more doable when we grasp just how wide and long and high and deep Christ's love is for us. I don't think we can truly find the love we're looking for until we first fall in love with the Author of love.

Sisters, Jesus spread His arms out to declare, "I love you *this* much." All He asks in exchange for His sacrifice is that we allow Him to dwell in our hearts.

The mistakes I've made in chasing relationships were mostly rooted in wanting to find someone who could play the leading role in the love story I wanted to write. There is no greater love story than the story of Jesus' birth, death, and resurrection. Want to know something else that's amazing? There are roles remaining to be filled in that story.

If you and a guy are "talking," but you aren't quite sure of what's next because he's hard to read, there's a role for you.

If you are dating a great man of God but sometimes forget that God's love is greater, there's a role for you.

If you have no guy, have had no guy, and doubt you'll ever have one, there's a role for you.

Whatever your relationship situation is, Jesus has a role for you in His love story. All you need to do to receive your part is go back to your first love. "For God so loved the world that he gave his one and only Son, that whoever believes in him shall not perish but have eternal life" (John 3:16).

God is your first love. He loved you before you existed. He loved you before your parents met. And He loved you so much that He gave His one and only Son, who fell for you with his arms opened wide and hands nailed to the cross. He fell for you in a painfully beautiful way. He fell for you in a way that no man ever has, or ever can.

Even if you've never pursued Him, He is your first love because He first loved you. He is your first love to go back to.

Falling in love with God is not just saying a pretty little prayer and "I love ya!" It's about devoting your life to Him and dancing with Him each morning. It's about treating God like you would a close friend by communicating with Him and doing every day with Him.

Let me tell you what will happen when you do that: God will not cheat on you or make you feel like garbage. He will not get tired of you and move on. He will not just somehow lose interest in you and quit talking to you. He's already seen you without makeup, knows what your morning breath smells like, and has been around you when you're PMSing—and He still loves you.

Go back to your first love, and God will love you faithfully, continually, and unfailingly.

Will I ever find a man to spend the rest of my life with? Oh goodness, I certainly hope so! I want to get married, and I truly believe that one day I will meet that man and he will talk so vividly about his first love that I feel God's presence in a new way simply by being with him.

My plan for finding the man of my dreams is to go back to my first love and allow Him to lead me to the man He has set aside for me.

My current relationship status is something I never thought I'd claim: "I don't need a man—I'm married to Jesus!"

Real Talk

- How does the idea of God as your "first love" make you feel?
- Has your desire for a relationship with a man ever come between you and experiencing God's love for you?
- What is your current relationship status?
- Read Romans 8:31–39. After reading this chapter, what does that passage mean to you?

LIE #9

Prayer is only for when you need help.

Chapter 24

Out of the Desert

"Oh my, you're the girl with the blog!"

That is how I was best known at my university. I giggled when I first heard it, but I haven't always liked being "the girl with the blog." I knew some of my fellow students didn't consider my blogging to be cool. Because I've been vocal about my faith through blogging, there were always people waiting for me to mess up. As you know by now, I've messed up plenty of times, so they didn't usually have to wait long. I've never claimed to be a person whose every action honors God. But I have persistently claimed to desire to live that kind of life.

On this particular night, the girl who recognized me was in the backseat of my car. I barely knew her, and I was driving her home from a fraternity party because she was drunk.

She took a gulp from my water bottle before continuing.

"So you always said, 'God said this, God said that.' I think I heard Him once at church camp in tenth grade. But I haven't heard Him since then, ya know? How do you even hear God?"

Before I could begin to answer, she switched subjects to venting about some guy who broke her heart. That lasted until I dropped her off at her dorm, and I didn't think she was in a good state for a theological conversation. Unfortunately, I forgot to get her name and didn't have a chance to follow up. I regret that.

Her question is important, because prayer is how we communicate with God, and if we don't know how to hear God, how are we to communicate with Him?

Dry Spells

First, let's address this lie that prayer is for when we need help. In one sense, that's actually true, if you operate under the belief that we *always* need God's help. But what this lie seeks to do is cause us to think that prayer is intended *only* for when we're in trouble and we need to cry out to God for help. That removes God from being part of our day-to-day walk.

God doesn't want to be reduced to just a 911, bail-me-out God. That's not much of a relationship. God desires regular communication between us and Him.

Except sometimes in my life, the communication hasn't always felt consistent. "Dry spell" is the phrase Christians like to use for what I'm talking about.

I remember one such period, in particular. In church on Sundays, people all around me had their hands raised, praising God during worship songs. Their eyes were closed and their body language made it seem like God was hanging with them more than He was hanging with me.

After a string of Sundays like that, I wondered if perhaps I wasn't good enough for God to listen to me. Or not good enough to hear God. Or maybe the people around me in church were better Christians than me, so God skipped over me and spoke to them.

The icing on the cake came when someone who had just become a Christian said: "God spoke to me. It was just so clear."

That didn't seem right to me. Did God actually speak to her? Over me? Come on—I'd been praying and waiting, and praying and waiting, and she had just found faith and apparently was already hearing from God. Who let her cut in line ahead of me? Where was my burning bush? Or my tingly feelings because Jesus was so alive inside of me?

My jealousy was wrong. Comparing my faith to hers only made things worse.

Dry seasons happen, and not just to me. Chances are, you've had some too. We revel in those times when we feel so connected to God that it's as though every thought and action occur so naturally and feel so spiritually right that we can visualize ourselves 100 percent immersed in God.

Then there are other times. I've gotten mad at God when He didn't seem to be speaking to me like He had previously, or when He was not being crystal clear in His directions for me. Truthfully, there have been times when I've considered God to be almost as bad of a communicator as my ex-boyfriend. I felt like every time I asked God to appear, He would reply only with the dreaded "K."

Like, come on God! That won't do. I need more!

Here is what I have learned, though, from that dry season and others: when the connection isn't as it should be, the problem is on my end, not God's.

The truth is that we are good enough for God to speak to. He wants us to run to Him eagerly and kneel at His feet. He cries out for us, as His children, to notice Him, embrace Him, and praise Him.

If you're not worshiping Him like others on a Sunday morning, He still cares for you. If you have been struggling to keep your Bible study commitment, He still cares for you. If you keep finding yourself wanting what the world offers, He still cares for you. If you went too far in your previous relationship, yes, He still cares for you.

If you've sinned, He wants you to come to Him, repent, and strive every day to do life with Him.

But don't be surprised if another dry season comes your way. As much as we want to avoid them, they are easy to slip into.

Distractions can cause a dry season. We allow ourselves to be distracted by the world's offerings and take our focus off of Christ. I've gone through periods when I focused more on trying to look hot than seeking Christ. I've prioritized working out so I'd have a spring break bod over digging deeper into God's Word. By the way, the things that distract us usually turn out to be temporary idols.

Busyness can also bring on a dry season. We get so busy with our schedules that we don't take time to communicate with God. Make daily prayer and Bible study priorities. As much as this hurts to realize, we usually find a way to accomplish the things we consider a priority. That means what we aren't accomplishing is not a priority. So schedule time each day to be alone with God.

It helps me to keep communication with God a priority when I think about how it's a priority for Him. One of the cool things about God being omnipresent is that He is always right there beside each and every one of us. We might not notice Him, but that doesn't mean He's avoiding us or just chilling or on break. In fact, when we don't notice Him, He is working behind the scenes to direct our individual love stories.

Sometimes we don't realize that God might be working differently than we're accustomed to and thus, we haven't noticed Him yet. That could be His strategy for revealing Himself in new ways to us.

Regardless of whether we notice Him or not, He's there and always available to talk with His children. My mom was eager to receive phone calls from me when I went off to college for the first time. God is waiting for His children to call Him even more than a college freshman's mom!

Hearing God

The girl I drove home asked how I could "hear" God.

If she could have understood me, I would have answered by telling her that we don't have to "hear" God to hear God. In fact, few people ever hear God speak in an actual voice. God has many ways of speaking to us that we don't hear.

Of course, since this is a chapter on prayer, we'll start with God speaking through prayer. His Holy Spirit can speak through "impressions"—like the times written about in this book when it felt like God was whispering into my heart. Sometimes we say we have a gut feeling, and I believe the Spirit puts that feeling in us. God speaks into our minds as we study the Bible and read devotionals.

God speaks through other believers. But be careful with this one. Just because a believer says "God told me to tell you" doesn't mean what he or she says is true. Anything that God tells you through another believer absolutely must, in every conceivable way, line up with the principles of Scripture.

God speaks through music and art. He sometimes speaks through circumstances. Another word of caution: circumstances will never override the truth of God's Word. Also, when God does speak through circumstances, He tends to confirm His message through other means.

God speaks through His creation. The fingerprints of God are everywhere.

> The heavens declare the glory of God; the skies proclaim the work of his hands. Day after day they pour forth speech; night after night they reveal knowledge. They have no speech, they use no words; no sound is heard from them. Yet their voice goes out into all the earth, their words to the ends of the world. In the heavens God has pitched a tent for the sun. (Psalm 19:1–4)

I often hear God when I hike and see mountains or listen to a child's giggle. I sense His presence when a cute puppy licks the end of my nose. I often think we complicate God's voice. Yes, you may hear Him through a big trial or through an obvious moment. However, we serve a good God who is in every moment of our lives, big or small. Maybe all you need is fresh air, silence, and five minutes staring at the ocean to remind you He is present. Maybe you need to be present in the everyday adventure in order for you to see God in your everyday.

God communicates in many ways, He knows how you're wired, and He knows the most effective and faith-building way to communicate with you.

In the 1990s, a pastor and counselor named Gary Chapman

wrote a book called *The 5 Love Languages: The Secret to Love that Lasts*. The book is still popular, with more than 11 million copies sold. In it, Chapman identified five love languages: words of affirmation, physical touch, quality time, receiving gifts, and acts of service. Chapman said that every person has one primary love language and one secondary love language, and identifying your partner's love languages produces better communication between couples.

I believe that the concepts behind those five love languages in Chapman's book also apply to the different ways we hear and sense God. Although Chapman uses the love languages to talk about romantic relationships, I believe we use these same languages to communicate with God. The following are questions to help you determine your primary and secondary "Jesus love languages":

1. "Words"

Do you sense God's presence when you write to Him in your journal? Do you hear Him clearer with a pen in your hand? When you listen to sermons, does it help you to take notes on what you are learning?

2. "Touch"

Do you feel closest to God through physical acts of worship, such as raising your hands in praise? Do you like to kneel or lie on the floor when you pray?

3. "Time"

Does the peace and quiet of stillness open up conversation between you and the Lord? Do you sense Him most when you eliminate distractions and focus on Him in prayer?

4. "Gifts"

Does God feel closest to you when you notice the gifts He has provided, whether the beauty of mountains, a sister's hug, or a simple phone call with a best friend? Do you feel Him more when you give up your favorite things for Him—like a day without texting or a month without pizza? Maybe giving God your Friday nights for a month and spending time with only Him can help your faith. Maybe forfeiting your Facebook for a season can help you with your dry season. Maybe you're sitting on the beach, and instead of Instagraming the waves, you listen to them and admire God's gift in nature.

Whether you embrace one of His gifts or give Him one of your worldly possessions, I've found this can be helpful in one's personal walk with God.

5. "Service"

Do you feel God most when using your hands and feet to build His kingdom? Do you hear Him when serving lunch to the homeless? Does the idea of serving God—either locally or abroad—sound like a good way for you to grow in relationship with Him in a new and powerful way?

If God doesn't seem there to you, I suggest you try a different Jesus love language than you usually use to communicate with God. Allow the Creator to speak to you in a variety of ways. If we box God in by assuming He can speak only through words, then we are denying that God is God.

Dry seasons are reminders to have faith in God. Faith is needed for what we can't detect with our senses—what we don't hear or see or feel.

Because of increased security in air travel, it's common to enter and exit a plane without seeing the pilot and copilot. We have faith that they're on the other side of the locked cockpit door and in command of the plane, but we can't see them.

In most cases, the devices that move an elevator up and down a building are not visible when we step inside the car for a ride. Faith that what is unseen is actually there is what leads us to push the button for our destination.

Have faith that God is working even when you can't sense Him, don't feel moved by a worship song, or find doubts about your enough-ness creeping into your thoughts.

Keep praying and keep seeking Him. Keep having faith. He desires to listen to your prayers. He wants to hear about your trials, heartaches, long days, and financial problems. He wants to hear you admit when you are struggling with your faith. He wants vulnerability from you.

And He wants you to come to Him even when you're not in trouble, because He wants to talk with you as a friend.

Real Talk

- When was the last time you encountered a "dry season"? How long did it last? What do you think caused it to end?
- What "Jesus love language" best describes you?
- How would you answer the question, "How do you even hear God?"
- Plan a time tomorrow to try out a new love language with God. Afterward, make note of how you heard Him differently and what He said to you.

Chapter 25

Mean What You Pray

I used to not really enjoy praying. I made praying too difficult, because I wanted to use eloquent words as I spoke to God. I wanted to sound smart.

That was evident when I was called upon to pray in front of a group of people, I thought.

How can I reference Scripture and add pretty words to sound like a good Christian?

I came up with a list of good-sounding phrases:

- "Lord, touch everyone's heart . . ."
- "Lord, may we be the hands and feet . . ."
- "Lord, let my life sing your praise . . ."
- "Lord, take me as I am . . ."
- "Lord, I'm doing great, but bless her heart—she needs *Jesus* . . . ." (Obviously, imagine this being said in a judgmental, self-righteous tone.)

I reached a point where I realized I was praying to my peers instead of to God.

Prayers should begin, "Dear Father"—not, "Dear Brittany in the pretty jumpsuit who usually sits next to me at church." Not, "Dear worship leader who I want to think I'm a Proverbs 31 kind of woman."

In the past, I prayed more to look like a good Christian than to become an obedient disciple. I prayed more out of selfish ambition than to grow closer to God. I used Scripture-based phrases, but I said those pretty phrases for the benefit of my reputation instead of for the purpose God had given me.

Even when I prayed alone, with nobody around to impress, my prayers weren't authentic. I prayed pretty prayers and asked God to use my hands and feet when I should have been praying:

- "Lord, You know I don't want to talk to the annoying woman at work. But give me the grace and love to do so."
- "Lord, You know I am struggling to keep my quiet time. I pray for the self-control to do so, and the eagerness to make me more excited about hanging out with you."
- "Lord, You and I both know I'm texting a guy who isn't good for me. I pray that I stop allowing myself to make up excuses to talk to him and finally end this."
- "Lord, You know that almost-relationships really hurt me. The man I thought liked me ghosted me. That one guy went from caring about me to not caring at all, and now I feel worthless. Although I know I'm not worthless, it is hard for me to believe it. I pray that I am reminded that my worth comes from You, and that I can lean on Your Scripture even when I don't feel like it."

- "Lord, I am struggling and I know she is too. I pray for both of us to grow closer to You and that our actions reflect a love for You."

We are a make-believe generation. We want to make believe that everything is okay.

"Oh, Christianity is easy," we say. We tell God, "Yeah, I've got it covered. Let me say the routine words and move on."

We don't have it covered. Our social media might say we're "fine" and life is "great." If we post we are fine frequently enough, perhaps we'll come to half believe it.

We know the truth, though. We know how we feel. We know what makes us hurt, what we feel our lives are missing, and what fruits of the Spirit we need more of in our lives.

Why, if our generation knows the truth, don't we admit the truth?

I totally get that's it difficult to admit the truth to peers. I'm guilty of that. But your eternal Father already knows how you feel. He knows how hard you're taking the breakup. He knows you feel left out at work. He knows how distant you feel from your husband. He knows your view of love is impacted by your parents' divorce. God knows all your fears, desires, trials, and temptations.

There's a parable I love that Jesus tells about a Pharisee praying compared with a tax collector praying. Pharisees were the religious leaders back in that time period, but they often struggled with pride—like many of us do today. Tax collectors were "obvious sinners." They often stole money and were known for being bad people. These men were obviously different in occupation and social standing. The way they prayed was different as well:

To some who were confident of their own righteousness and looked down on everyone else, Jesus told this parable: "Two men went up to the temple to pray, one a Pharisee and the other a tax collector. The Pharisee stood by himself and prayed: 'God, I thank you that I am not like other people—robbers, evildoers, adulterers—or even like this tax collector. I fast twice a week and give a tenth of all I get.' But the tax collector stood at a distance. He would not even look up to heaven, but beat his breast and said, 'God, have mercy on me, a sinner.' I tell you that this man, rather than the other, went home justified before God. For all those who exalt themselves will be humbled, and those who humble themselves will be exalted." (Luke 18:9–14)

Do you see the difference in their prayers? I do. The Pharisee was praying self-righteously. He prayed to brag, to share his resume, and to make it seem like he was the greatest man to ever walk the planet. However, the tax collector, who was considered a "bad man" by society, prayed differently. He was humble. He was vulnerable. He admitted his flaws and admitted that he needed God.

I want to encourage you to be more real with God when you pray. Be vulnerable. I mean, if we can't be vulnerable with God, who knows everything about us, then how can we expect to be vulnerable with our peers, who know little more about us other than our fake "fine"? How can you glorify God without humbling yourself?

Stop playing make-believe. Instead, believe in the power of authentic prayer and vulnerability. Sit at Jesus' feet and tell Him about your day, your relationship problems, your bills coming due, and your crazy dreams. Talk to Him when life is great and you're driving down the road jamming to the songs of your teenage years.

And don't be afraid to tell Him when you're angry, hurt, and life isn't all sunshine.

Psalm 102:17 says, "He will respond to the prayer of the destitute; he will not despise their plea."

The psalmists knew how to pray!

Real Talk

- When praying in public, do you pray more to be heard by peers than by God?
- Do you feel like you can be vulnerable during your prayers? Why or why not?
- What is on your heart as you read this chapter? What have you been afraid to admit to yourself or God?
- Pray and tell God about your struggles, whether you think they are too small for Him to care or too big to be conquered.

Chapter 26

Time Best Spent

*M*y friend wanted to celebrate her twenty-first birthday by inviting friends to a burger-and-bar restaurant downtown. We exchanged a series of fifteen happy birthday greetings and bought a picture from an overpriced photo booth. I barely knew most of her friends.

I wound up talking with a girl I'll call Denise. She read my blog, so we had an easy starting point for our conversation. Denise described herself as being in an I-don't-know-what-to-do-with-my-life funk. I think the clinical name is Early Twenties-itis.

Denise was smart, with two difficult degrees from Baylor's business school. She had received a top internship the previous summer from a company that potentially could offer her a job. As a journalism major, I envied her knowing that after graduation, she was in line for a well-paying job no matter where she landed.

Denise wasn't as confident of her future as I was. She wasn't sure if God had called her to be a light while working in a financially stable field or to be a counselor. Denise said she regretted

185

not majoring in psychology because she seemed bent more toward compassion than working with Excel sheets, big numbers, and budgets.

I started in with the whole "let me help you" thing.

"Maybe you could go to grad school." "Maybe you could intern at a counseling office your last semester and see if you like that field." "Maybe you could take the high-paying job for now and later use your finance degree to run a counseling center."

The advice flowed fairly easily, but I didn't think to offer the best thing I could do for her: pray. I didn't ask if she had been praying about her career, or suggest she should. I came up with lots of plans for her that sounded good to me, but I didn't once ask if she had talked to the One who knew her future.

I think my mistake is all too common in our generation. We've been told to chase what we want—chase the idealized American lifestyle, the dream we've held since we were ten, the career (or husband) that can provide us with the nice house in the gated community and the family cruise to the Bahamas during the Christmas holiday.

I'm not saying there is anything inherently wrong with those examples, but it *is* wrong to focus all our energy on chasing the things the world values—on making them our life's pursuit. Because when we do that, we leave Jesus out of the planning. I mean, it doesn't take much outside help to set our targets based on what everybody around us is either chasing or already has. When we focus on the wrong people, places, and possessions, we forget that our lives are meant to worship God. We instead worship the world's dreams and ideals.

When we come down with Early Twenties-itis, all the things we think we need to get done scream "Chase me!" So we chase the high GPA, making extra money from a side job, and occasionally eating a meal that isn't greasy and served out of a paper bag. We look for small gaps in our calendar to work out, have a social life, and—especially when our bank account drops below ten bucks—call our family to let them know we're still alive. And hungry.

But where in our calendars do we make room for stopping all the chasing so we can spend time at Jesus' feet?

Buzzfeed quizzes that tell us what *Gossip Girl* characters we are? Done. Research for a job to replace the frustrating one we have now? Done. Switch major for the third—and final, I promise Mom—time? Done.

Sit at Jesus' feet? I'll let you mark "Done" or not.

Luke 10:38–42 is, for me, one of the most convicting passages in the New Testament:

> As Jesus and his disciples were on their way, he came to a village where a woman named Martha opened her home to him. She had a sister called Mary, who sat at the Lord's feet listening to what he said. But Martha was distracted by all the preparations that had to be made. She came to him and asked, "Lord, don't you care that my sister has left me to do the work by myself? Tell her to help me!"
>
> "Martha, Martha," the Lord answered, "you are worried and upset about many things, but few things are needed—or indeed only one. Mary has chosen what is better, and it will not be taken away from her."

I'm as Martha as it comes—detailing my Kate Spade planner out to the *n*th degree and getting annoyed when Mary doesn't even make, much less follow, a to-do list. Hey, I'd like to be over there sitting as Jesus' feet like her, just listening to Him. But there are so many things that need to be done this instant!

So many things that need to be done. Sound familiar?

Jesus told Martha that *few* things are needed. That includes spending time sitting at His feet.

Of course, we can't physically sit at Jesus' feet as Mary did in that story, but we can have the same effect through prayer.

I know it can get annoying to have a problem and seemingly always be told, "Just pray about it." Perhaps that's annoying because, deep down inside, we know it is the correct response. It's what we are called to do. Prayer grows our relationship with the Lord. Through prayer, He gives us wisdom.

Perhaps another reason the "just pray" answer is annoying is because we can't really pray for God's direction for our future without yielding what we want to what He wants.

Perhaps we are annoyed because when we pray, we are admitting we are dependent when we'd rather be independent. Isn't society pushing us to be more independent? Especially us ladies?

This can be a tough one for me. I often find myself saying, "Don't pray only when you need help." (Taking into account, as I stated earlier, that we always need God's help.)

I think most people get that they can pray in times of trouble. How many non-Christians do you know who post "will you pray for me/us/him/her?" when there's an illness, a lost job, or a death. But Jesus doesn't want to be just someone we run to when absolutely necessary. He wants us to spend time sitting at His feet.

Before you change your job or your major, change your habits and add regular prayer time to your schedule. We're not called to be independent or busy or always checking off boxes. We are called to be obedient.

Real Talk

- What in your life is currently worrying you?
- When was the last time you sat at Jesus' feet just to praise Him and spend time with Him?
- What scares you most about being dependent?
- What step can you take to schedule regular prayer time?
- Take time to pray honestly to God. Talk to Him as you would a friend. Visualize yourself sitting at His feet and telling Him about all your worries, fears, and questions.

LIE #10

You will never be enough.

Chapter 27

Strong Enough

Jena was my best friend. She was a special needs student at our high school, and we ate lunch together almost every day. Unfailingly loyal, she inspired me. Despite her limitations, I considered her a better person than I could ever be. My senior year, I asked her to be my prom "date."

She was diagnosed with cancer after I went off to college out of state, and I couldn't see her as often as I would have liked.

I vividly remember the day Jena's mother called to tell me that Jena wasn't doing well. Her mom put Jena on the phone so we could talk. Jena's speech was slurred. I could tell the cancer was winning. I didn't sleep well after that call. I prayed that God would allow me to get home and see her one more time before she died. Thankfully, I was able to see her for a whole week, spending much of that time sitting by her bed and listening to her cry in pain.

The illness stole Jena's everyday. Yes, she was in special needs classes before, but she was very much a normal teenage girl. She loved to talk, and she loved receiving stuffed animals. She loved shopping. In fact, we had similar styles. We both loved sparkles, which was why our prom dresses looked almost identical.

But in the months before her death, Jena's everyday was robbed by cancer. She became bedridden. She could no longer tell me stories at lunch. She could no longer call me and talk normally. The cancer caused her to lose function of her body. She was in pain. All she seemed to do was cry.

A month after that visit, I received a text from Jena's mom. I left my duplex and cried in the parking lot. My roommates joined me, wrapping their arms around me and crying with me.

Cancer had won.

My questions and doubts flowed: *Why would God let Jena have cancer, knowing her body wouldn't have the strength to overcome it? Why did He take my friend from me? Why couldn't He have made my friend strong enough to beat cancer? Why couldn't He have made me strong enough to handle this pain?*

"God gives His hardest battles to His strongest soldiers." That quote makes me mad. I've seen it on social media way too many times, pasted over a dramatic photo of a wave or dark, cloudy sky.

When Jena died, that quote made no sense. If that quote were true, then why did God give me the hard battle of losing Jena when I was not one of His strongest soldiers?

People tried to inspire me with that same quote when my family evacuated for Hurricane Katrina, when my self-image plummeted because of bullying, and when I got weighed down by insecurity. When I doubted God's existence, that quote was presented as the answer to my questions.

"God gives His hardest battles to His strongest soldiers."

False!

Weakness and Strength

Remember picking teams in middle school PE? I wish I could forget. Whether it was flag football or dodgeball or any other sport, I was always picked last.

I wore glasses from Walmart, a headband from Limited Too, and socks with frills on the ends. I'm pretty sure I wore pink Crocs and silly bands up my arms too. Everything about my appearance screamed "Weak!" to the middle school team captains, selecting their teams as if playing for an Olympic gold medal.

The only one I know who would pick a girl like me—who got her glasses from the same store where we bought the family mayonnaise—was God. Thank you, God! I'm actually a great draft choice for God, because he likes to pick the weak to show His strength.

Moses had a speech impediment, and he led God's people to the Promised Land. A young, unmarried woman named Mary gave birth to the Savior of the world. Peter had anger issues and denied Christ three times, yet he became a leading figure in spreading the gospel across the world. David was a small boy when he defeated Goliath. Jonah ran the other direction when called to preach about God to a people who were his enemies. Sarah was ninety when she bore her first son for Abraham, the father of all nations. Paul killed Christians before he shared the gospel with Gentiles and went to jail because he wouldn't stop spreading the gospel message.

I'd argue that the quote I mentioned earlier has it backward. It's more likely that God gives His hardest battles to the weakest soldiers so that He can use them to prove His strength.

We serve a God who chooses the unqualified to fulfill His plan, children as the example of the type of faith a disciple should have, rainy days to bring rainbows, and—I'd contend—you and me to be victorious in battles, all by the power of Jesus.

Me and My Stones

David and Goliath is one of my favorite Bible stories. You can read it in 1 Samuel 17, but here's a synopsis.

The Israelite and Philistine armies were prepared to square off in a battle when one member of the Philistine army offered to meet one of the Israelites one-on-one, winner-take-all. His name was Goliath, and he was a giant. None of the Israelites wanted to accept his challenge.

David wasn't old enough to belong to the Israelite army, but he said he would take on the giant with the Lord's help. King Saul supplied David with the king's pieces of armor and sent him off with a, "Go, and the Lord be with you." But David declined the armor, instead picking up five smooth stones for his slingshot.

When the combatants met on the battlefield, David killed Goliath with the first shot from his slingshot, gaining victory for the Israelites.

The reason this is one of my favorite stories is that David used a simple slingshot and stone to accomplish one of the most stunning military victories ever. He did so because with God, he had the power to win the battle.

I've faced battles in my life with what felt like five stones in my hand—and without confidence in the Lord. In those situations, I don't feel strong enough for the battle. My five stones make me feel weak compared to what I'm up against, and the best I know to do is turn and run. I'll say, "Really, God? I'm not strong enough."

You've probably had the same experience.

Disease, insecurity, family divorce, losing a job, failing a class, having less money in your savings account than the rent that's due in three days.

Those are all giants, and they make you look down with doubt to the five measly stones in your hand. The problem isn't the stones in your hand; it's the direction you're looking for strength.

David's confidence did not come from his strength, but God's. David's victory had nothing to do with how strong he was and everything to do with how strong God was. Don't look to your stones, but look to the all-powerful God who wants to armor you with His strength.

With Him, you are enough to march into battle. Any battle.

The summer camp I attended growing up had this sign over the gates to their boys' camp: "God gives us hills to climb and the strength to climb them."

Now that's a quote I like.

If we allow Him, God will supply us with the strength and power needed to overcome trials. The battles we face serve to prove His strength. We don't have to be strong soldiers to fight in His army, just soldiers. No modifier necessary. When we sign up for the fight, he supplies the modifier.

We are all weak soldiers on our own. But in His strength, we are strong enough for the most difficult battles.

So if you also have had to say goodbye to someone you love, rest in the truth that although God does give us more than we can handle, He will never give us more than He can handle. Lean on Him in your trials and there will be joy in the morning.

Real Talk

- Do you ever feel like you aren't Christian enough for God to use you? Why do you feel that way?
- Who is your favorite Bible character who was weak but accomplished much because of God's strength? What about that person's victory stands out to you?
- How can God use you and your weaknesses to bring Him glory?
- Write a prayer asking God to show His strength through your weakness.

Chapter 28

God's Love Letter

I've been vulnerable with you about my struggles growing up striving to be "pretty enough" for the world, knowing some of you need to relate to a woman who's endured the same battles you have.

At fourteen, I cried on picture day at school. I had a huge forehead and skin as white as Casper the Friendly Ghost. My hair was frizzy and my chest was as flat as an ironing board.

While shopping for my formal dress in college, I cried in the dressing room where no one could see me. Nothing about my body was flattering. I thought the reward for surviving puberty was a hot body. Not for me. I felt like a pregnant whale.

Looks tend to define worth in our society, and the pursuit of pretty enough never ends. Fast fashion demands you conform to a new trend every few weeks. It depletes your bank account and feeds into ruthless cycles of emotional poverty as you constantly strive to fit a rapidly changing standard. And the major corporations only get greedier for wealth and greedier for your adherence to their lies.

One of my high school classmates got a nose job for her sixteenth birthday. Friends in college refused to go to any formal without wearing Spanx or participating in a juice cleanse the week before so they would look skinny in their dresses. Women in their thirties and forties buy expensive wrinkle creams to hide the fact that they are undergoing the completely normal human process called aging.

Across generations, women struggle with feeling they aren't pretty enough.

Uniquely Me

My turning point came when I realized I would never be pretty enough by the world's standards. I would never have super model legs. I would never be a size 0 again—and wouldn't want to. And I would never have size DD boobs.

I could accept all that because I finally grasped what mattered most: God did not create me to be like anyone else. He created me to be uniquely me—the only me He created. I can't begin to describe the freedom I experienced when I fully comprehended that I am God's daughter, handcrafted in my mother's womb.

Recognizing the lies our society promotes and resting in the following truth He has spoken into me brought me security in my appearance I'd never felt before. During my sophomore year of college, I wrote a letter from God to me. I finally found Him again and this time I promised myself I wouldn't walk away:

Dear Daughter,

I know your thoughts. When you stand in front of the mirror and complain that your hair is "too thin," your thighs "too large," and your nose "weirdly shaped," I hear those thoughts. I know your thoughts about your stomach and the pimples that seem to worsen when it's your time of the month. I hear you say you want a bigger butt and a smaller waist. I see you stalk random people on social media who look like you wish you looked. I hear you compare yourself to other girls. I even heard your tears the night the guy broke your heart and you thought it was because you were not pretty enough.

I hear it all. And, My child, it breaks My heart.

I know you think you are not pretty enough. But I did not create you to be enough for the world. I did not create you for this world. I created you for something greater than getting 100 likes on your selfies. I created you for something more important than having an attractive guy comment the fire emoji on your bikini picture. I created you to be in relationship with Me, your heavenly Father. I created you to find joy in your purpose, not how you look on a Friday night.

When I designed you, I handcrafted you in the image of Me. No other creation was designed that way. The roses, mountains, oceans, and puppies were not designed in My image like you are. You were knit together perfectly in the womb. You are My favorite creation, yet you still look in the mirror and cry. You complain about your lack of beauty, you complain about the way I handcrafted you. Yet you are My most beautiful creation, My greatest masterpiece.

I designed you. Every part of you. Even that piece of hair in the corner of your head that never straightens. Even the freckles you try to cover. I created your body shape and your hair. I created you not to be gawked at by guys, but to reflect My image for all around you to see.

You have been told that you are ugly. You have heard comments insecure girls have made about your physical appearance. A guy dumped you and you were so sure it was because you gained a few pounds.

My child, they were wrong. The world is wrong. The world tells you that you are not pretty enough. I say you are altogether beautiful. The world tells you that you look better when you hide your face with makeup. I say I created you in My image. The world tells you that life is better if you look like a model. I say that you find joy in life only when you walk with Me.

The truth is, you are beautiful and created the way you are for a reason. You are My greatest artwork. You are My child. Every inch of you is beautiful, and your ability to walk with Me is your greatest gift.

Know the worth I have given you, My child. Know that you may never be pretty enough by the world's standards, but you are more than pretty enough for Me. Your purpose is your greatest accessory.

Cling to Me, and I will give you joy. Your physical beauty is temporary. Your body is not eternal. Everything around you is temporary, except Me. Start doing life with Me more. Stop focusing on new ways to quickly lose weight. Instead, open your Bible, pray to Me, and hang out with Me. Your beauty will not be with you forever. I will.

You may not feel beautiful. But I, who hung the stars and painted the seas, made you in My image, and that is beautiful.

You are Mine,

God

Why You're Beautiful

I once heard this quote: "Tell a girl she is beautiful, she will believe it for a moment. Tell a girl she is ugly, she will believe it for a lifetime."

For years, I was proof of the quote's accuracy, because I allowed a group of bullies to determine how I viewed myself. Even to this day, I sometimes hear their insults in my memory.

"Grace, your forehead is so big it could be an airport. I swear planes could land on it."

"Grace, you'll never get a boyfriend. You're not the look guys want."

I know now that they were wrong. But so is that quote, because it fails to account for what God can do when a girl lets the One who designed her determine her worth.

Here's a quote that is true: "I am beautiful not because of *who* I am, but *whose* I am." Memorize that. A woman will never be completely at peace with her looks until she believes that.

The world offers us makeup to be prettier, push-up bras to be sexier, and fad diets to give us confidence. God offers the truth that He created us and has declared us beautiful—and that is a fact to celebrate.

We've talked a lot about looks in this book. It has been a years-long battle for me, and through comments on my blog, I know it's a widespread source of stress for many.

To the girl who is insecure and finds herself frustrated when she looks in the mirror, I am sorry you are going through that.

To the girl who has gone somewhere in a nice dress and still not felt pretty enough, I've been there.

And to the girl who has been told she is ugly, I've suffered that pain too.

I'm praying for all of you—praying that you and I will remember our Creator holds the world in His hand and holds us near to His heart. You are loved. You are worthy. God says so.

Early in this book, I challenged you to take your book to the mirror. I want you to do that again. Now, look into the mirror and say this: "Thank you, God, for creating me as You did. I have decided to celebrate Your artwork." Say that every morning until you're saying it with conviction.

Real Talk

- As we near the end of this book, what do you think now of the world's "pretty enough" standards?
- What do you think God thinks of you?
- Pray and thank God for creating you as a unique masterpiece. Ask Him to remove your insecurities and help you see yourself the way He sees you.

Chapter 29

At a Moment's Notice

I went through CPR and Heimlich Maneuver training four times. Not because I was a slow learner, but because the camp where I worked each summer insisted that its staff be fully prepared for a situation that would require executing those life-saving techniques.

I took the classes seriously. I can be a worrier, and although I knew the chance of using those techniques was small, the chance did exist. We never knew when we might be called on to save a child's life.

Fortunately, I never had to perform CPR or the Heimlich on a camper.

But I did have to put my training to use on a friend at the mall.

Sophie, Haylee, and I ordered three of the largest Great American Cookies cakes for a pool party for our campers. While the cakes were being made, we went to the food court for lunch.

During our meal, Haylee stood and grabbed her throat. I heard a gasp, and the look on her face indicated something wasn't right.

"You okay?" I asked, then took another bite of my chicken nuggets.

Haylee didn't answer. Her face started turning purple and she gasped for air.

"What do we do?!?" Sophie yelled, arms flailing.

In our CPR and Heimlich classes, we learned that we have about ten seconds to decide if we should act. I knew I was in that ten-second window.

I thought, *What if I do something wrong?*

Putting that fear aside, I stood, wrapped my arms around Haylee in the proper Heimlich position, and began performing the technique as trained. I alternated between the pat on the back and the thrusts into the abdomen that basically lifted her off the ground.

Two chunks of food flew out of her mouth.

The three of us looked at each other in shock. We laughed, but we were low-key scared.

I needed a few seconds to process what had happened. I had just used what I'd learned on dummies to help a real person—a close friend of mine, at that. I had possibly saved Haylee's life.

As Christians, we encounter so many moments where we have to decide whether to use what we have been trained to do. Moments where God calls us to pick up our crosses. Moments where God can use our gifts and talents to build His kingdom.

When those moments come to you, are you going to make them count? Or will you look away and hope someone else fills the need?

We must be prepared to answer when called. If we miss out on spreading the gospel message, we are missing an opportunity to bring others into the kingdom with us.

The gospel is so real to me that the idea of not spreading it to those who need the truth scares me. The idea of leaving someone I encounter without giving them an opportunity to experience my Savior is frightening. I desire to use every chance I receive to love others and introduce them to God's love.

Because we are Christians, we know the truth that results in life transformation. We know what we are called to do. "Go therefore and make disciples of all nations, baptizing them in the name of the Father and of the Son and of the Holy Spirit, teaching them to observe all that I have commanded you" (Matthew 28:19–20a, ESV).

We know, but it's still difficult. The thought of putting into practice what we've learned can be intimidating. It's a lot easier to raise our hands in church and say we're ready to witness to our neighbor than it is to walk out the doors and follow through.

But what is the gospel worth if it does not affect our actions?

What good is it, my brothers, if someone says he has faith but does not have works? Can that faith save him? If a brother or sister is poorly clothed and lacking in daily food, and one of you says to them, "Go in peace, be warmed and filled," without giving them the things needed for the body, what good is that? So also faith by itself, if it does not have works, is dead. But someone will say, "You have faith and I have works." Show me your faith apart from your works, and I will show you my faith by my works. You believe that God is one; you do well. Even the demons believe—and shudder! (James 2:14–19, ESV)

Friends, we can't show our faith without having a desire to change the evil we see in the world. We can't love our neighbor's

Creator and not love our neighbor. Loving God means loving people. Loving God means living a life led by the Spirit. Loving God with a genuine heart causes you to empathize with others, dress yourself in compassion, and bear fruit wherever you go.

Loving God means getting up in times of trouble and taking action even when it's scary.

Haylee's life depended on me in the food court. But you have a chance to impact someone's eternity.

If you know a friend or family member who is spiritually "choking," stand up and take action. Be bold. You can do this!

Real Talk

- Have you had a moment where you felt called to help your neighbor? How did you respond to that call?
- Why is living for God important?
- What can you pray for in order to become a better servant?
- Pray that you will recognize opportunities around you to fulfill the Great Commission of Matthew 28.

Chapter 30

The "I Am" Life

O ur journey is almost complete. Before we say goodbye, I'd like for us to look back over the ground we've covered together. Let's call these sixty-five tips for living the "I Am" life:

1. At the gates to heaven, you won't be asked if you were in a top-tier sorority. You won't be asked if you hung out with the cool people at work. And your popularity in the world won't earn you any points. Not even Jesus was popular with the world, and He was perfect.
2. Numbers do not define you.
3. That includes the numbers in your grades.
4. That also includes the numbers on the scale.
5. And your rating out of ten on the "hot scale."
6. Not even if you can bench press 200 pounds. (@ all the guys at the gym—you need to chill.)
7. There is no shame in innocence. Or in making mistakes. But learn from your mistakes. Mistakes can be lessons that

prove to be big blessings. Use your mistakes to gain wisdom. Then with that wisdom, pray each morning to make choices that please the Lord.

8. Your metabolism is not what it used to be, and it will keep heading in the wrong direction. That's okay.

9. You won't always understand what God is doing, but remember: He has a plan. Trust Him.

10. Every person you meet is battling something.

11. Life isn't always filled with great moments.

12. It takes climbing to reach the mountaintop.

13. That girl you stalk? You know her Instagram feed, not her life. You're seeing the highlight reel, not the entire game.

14. A broken heart is temporary; it's not permanently damaged.

15. Another guy can't put the pieces back together.

16. Neither can a night on the town.

17. Neither can ice cream. (But it can totally help.)

18. Only God can restore a broken heart.

19. Stop texting your ex. *Ex* means former. There's a reason (or reasons) he's an ex.

20. Loving Jesus means loving people.

21. Loving Jesus also means loving the image of Him in your mirror.

22. Stop hiding your emotions. Don't cry behind locked doors. You have people in your life who care about you. Cry on their shoulders.

23. God cares about you. Cry to Him.

24. Suicide is *never* the answer.

25. Breathe in, breathe out until you feel better.

26. Is your heart beating? That's a sign that you are here for a purpose. Your life is no mistake.

27. Just because you doubt doesn't mean you don't believe in Jesus.

28. Don't choose a career based on money.

29. You can use any passion or gift to serve a purpose bigger than yourself if you give it back to the One who gave it to you.

30. You do not need pretty prayers for God to listen.

31. Talk to God like you're talking to a friend. You are.

32. Look for the good in everyone.

33. That includes the mean girl nobody likes. She's mean for a reason, probably because someone has been mean to her. Overwhelm her with kindness.

34. Pray to have the Lord's eyes and you'll love the people you see.

35. Pray to have the Lord's hands and you'll reach out to others.

36. Pray to have the Lord's feet and go where He calls you.

37. A bad day does not equal a bad life.

38. You don't need six-pack abs to find a man who will genuinely love you.

39. You need a spouse who will look at you when you're eighty, wrinkled, and a little chunky and still love you. If he loves you now because of your body and hair, that's not real love. Looks fade. Find someone who will love you like Jesus. Their love for you won't fade.

40. Do some squats. Go for a run. Eat fresh fruit. But do it to feel healthy, not to attract a guy.

41. You are never too old to find a new hobby.

42. You were beautiful before someone told you that you were.

43. If you are confused as to whether you are in a relationship with him, you're not. Leave. You deserve clarity, not insecurity.

44. You deserve friendships that are mutual.

45. Some of the best Friday nights are spent with food and a puppy. It is okay to not always be social.

46. Stop worrying about whether your crush will text you back. If he doesn't, that's his loss.

47. In general, stop overanalyzing everything.

48. Pray for your future spouse.

49. Pray for your future bridesmaids.

50. Something to look forward to: there's a good chance you have yet to meet some of the most influential people you'll have in your life.

51. Storms bring strength.

52. Storms also bring rainbows. Persevere and keep watching.

53. Stop Pinteresting your dream life and start living it.

54. The Bible is extremely relatable. Study it.

55. Romans 8:28: "And we know that in all things God works for the good of those who love him, who have been called according to his purpose." God is on your team. He has a purpose for you greater than your bad day. He wants you to have moments to celebrate.

56. Never forget what Jesus did for you on the cross. His death was brutal and painful. It was ugly, and it was love. Don't allow that truth to ever become numb to you, no matter how many times you hear the story.

57. Carbs are good.

58. Get to know someone you look up to.

59. Keep in mind that someone looks up to you. Act like the woman you want your children to become.

60. Insecurity is real and life is hard. But if you lock your eyes on your Maker, you can experience joy.

61. Never forget that your worth comes from God and the fact that He created you.
62. Read good books.
63. God turns ashes into beauty and trials into testimonies.
64. God wants to dance with you. Stop dancing with the world. Begin to follow God's lead.
65. Cue the music.

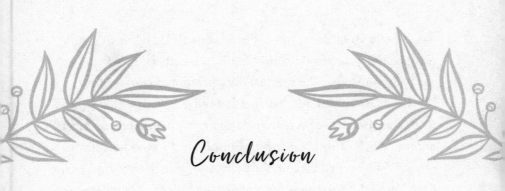

Conclusion

Who Will You Dance With?

Here we are—the final song! Thanks for the time you have shared with me. It's important that we women stick together.

It's not easy being us, is it? Life hurts sometimes. Whatever areas of your life you opened this book wanting to change—or learned you need to work on as you've read—I wish this final chapter could contain special powers that would instantly grant your wishes. But this book contains no special powers.

However, it does contain truth that refutes the lies the world pounds you with, persistently telling you that you're "not enough" in order to separate you from the life God designed for you. Have you had enough of those lies? I have! And I hope you've decided after reading this book that you'll cling tightly to the Lord.

Remember this line from the first chapter: Life is a dance, and the most important question we will answer is, "Who will we dance with?"

We follow the lead of the one we choose to dance with.

If you search for validation through social media, beauty,

money, or relationships, you will find yourself led by them. Those are temporary satisfactions that result in heartbreaks and tears in the bathroom. They distract you from pursuing God.

I've been bullied and lonely. I've been so insecure that I mistreated my body. I've been dropped to my knees by a broken heart and the death of my best friend. But each time my knees hit the ground, I discovered I was in the perfect position to pray. And each time I prayed, I sensed my heavenly Father asking, "Daughter, can I have this dance?"

The moment I let go of the world and took God's hand to dance with Him, I found joy. I found life and acceptance. I found beauty in everyday miracles. When I saw a mountaintop, I saw evidence of His creative power. When I woke up, I realized my opportunity to discover more of my purpose. When I looked in the mirror, I recognized a masterpiece made in the Creator's image.

I accepted God's outstretched hand and followed Him step by step. He took me to new heights and new challenges. He took me on a journey of grace and elegance.

As I danced with God, I locked my eyes on Him. I lost sight of worldly desires. I smiled a smile not just of happiness, but of joy. Others noticed how fulfilled I was, and they wanted to join in.

If you are fighting against insecurities, regret, and pain—listen. Listen to the tender whisper of the Father. He is the One you are created to please, not the world. He is offering you His hand for a beautiful dance into eternity.

Will you dance with Him? Will you release your grip on this world?

I pray you will allow the Father to cut in.

Ten truths the world doesn't want you to know:

1. You are beautiful because God created you in His image.
2. God gives His love to you freely—you don't have to (and can't) earn it.
3. Your past does not define you. God can turn your trials into testimonies.
4. Your purpose is to reflect God as you love those around you.
5. The most important number is *one*: For God so loved the world that He gave His one and only Son. . . .
6. Your weakness presents an opportunity for God to display His strength.
7. God writes the best love stories.
8. God wants to be your closest friend.
9. Prayer is for when you need help—and you always need God's help. So always pray.
10. You *are* enough. God says you are.

Acknowledgments

During my sophomore year of college, I felt called to write a book. *Called* is such a cheesy line, I know, but there's no other way to describe what happened in my heart other than hearing the Lord call me to scribble the words you are reading. Throughout this process I quickly learned I could not do this alone. I did not do this alone.

- ❧ To my parents and brother, thank you. Thank you for raising me in the church and being supportive. And I'm sorry for my crazy teenage years.
- ❧ To my grandmother Valentine, thank you for being my biggest supporter and teaching me the importance of being poised and kind. I learn more about Jesus every time we are together.
- ❧ To Stacy Ellefson, my mentor and friend, thank you. You were the first person I told I wanted to write a book, and you said, "*I see it!*" You believed in me and my crazy dream. Thank you.
- ❧ To Mrs. Liz Vinteruella and Anna Mahr, your stories of

strength helped make this book what it is. Thank you for sharing and for your wisdom.

⚘ To Catherine DeArmas, thank you for inviting me into your home when I was broke and pushing me to live a life of ministry. You truly are the big sister I never had.

⚘ To my agent, Chip, thank you for believing in me every step of the way. You took a chance on a college student. I can't thank you enough for that.

⚘ To my team at W Publishing, thank you for your wisdom and hard work. I admire you greatly and am honored to bring God glory alongside y'all.

⚘ To my college roommates, Lauren, Britta, Dresden, and Nora—thank you for being there every single step of the way. Thank you for our many nights of girl talk. Thank you for seeing my tears and encouraging me when I was down. Thank you for being the kind of friends who could make me laugh and who would cry with me. As we prepare to separate and move into that scary thing called adulthood, I pray we continue to encourage each other to chase crazy dreams, workout every now and then, eat good carb-loaded food, and most importantly to seek Him. You guys saw me at my worst, yet you loved me through it all.

⚘ To all my friends from Camp Crestridge and all my old counselors—thank you for being more than summer friends and mentors. Each of the friendships and mentors I gained through those years have made me better.

⚘ To all my readers, thank you. You push me to keep writing. Keep seeking Him—even when it is hard.

⚘ To Baylor University, you helped me grow in my walk with the Lord and gave me friendships that will last forever. I will always be proud to be a Baylor bear. Thank you Baylor University.

❧ To Taylor Swift, thank you. Whether you see this or not, your music was the soundtrack played through every stage of my life. You taught me to fall in love with vulnerability and storytelling. I couldn't sing . . . so I decided to write a book.

❧ To the girl holding this book, thank you. You are the reason I write. Chances are you are holding this book because you are at least curious about Jesus. Be curious. Chase adventure. And most importantly, dance with Jesus.

❧ Most importantly, thank you to Jesus Christ. You took my debt and paid it all. You loved me when I didn't deserve it. You taught me there is more to life than this world. You kept leaving the 99 to bring me, just one sheep, back home. You cared for me, gave me purpose, and taught me life is about dancing with you. You transformed my life. Thank you for your pursuit of me, and I love dancing with you.

And to my heartbreaks, failures, joys, and embarrassing moments—thank you. Every trial of my past has shaped the outcome of my future. Every moment of weakness allowed me to find strength in the Lord. And through every season, the good and the bad, I was able to learn that God is constant in a life that is ever-changing.

My prayer is that the Lord is present in the thoughts and hearts of every woman who reads this book. I pray this book helps women know more about the Lord. I pray this book pushes women to find their worth in Jesus. Most importantly, I pray for more women to know that Jesus says we are enough.

About the Author

Grace Valentine is a popular blogger who founded the Enough Movement. Her readers love the fact that she is young, ordinary, and relatable—they say her fresh voice helps them navigate their own faith and life. Grace's mission is to help those who have struggled like she has to find their worth in Someone who truly is worth following.

Grace graduated from Baylor University in 2018 with a degree in Journalism. She is currently the Content and Curriculum Coordinator for the student ministry of First Baptist Orlando in Orlando, Florida.